THE CRUMBLES STORY

STORY

A Tale of Eastbourne's
Colourful Heritage

ANN BOTHA
ALB Books

The ancient beachland known as the Crumbles that fronts the levels of Eastbourne and Pevensey has an atmosphere and quality uniquely its own. This book is dedicated to all those who knew and valued its strange beauty in the past and to those who will live there in the future.

First published in 1996 by S.B. Publications
© 1996 Ann Botha

This edition published 2006 by ALB Books, 7 Fraser Avenue, Eastbourne, East Sussex BN23 6BB
© 2006 Ann Botha

0-9553475-0-5 (ISBN 10)
978-0-9553475-0-4 (ISBN 13)

Design & Digital Artwork: ian@thecreativeplot.com
Print: Paul Green Printing, Faber House, 94 Wallis Road, London E9 5LN. 020 8986 9511

CONTENTS

INTRODUCTION

How did it all begin? This question has universal appeal for every subject under the sun and the story of the Crumbles at Eastbourne unfolds a history which stretches back over centuries.

My own fascination with the Crumbles began some twenty years ago when a casual walk on a warm summer morning took me to the shingle land so near to my home. There I found that in a few short weeks a windswept stretch of pebbles had been transformed into a brilliant garden of wild flowers. I stayed there for hours that day and quite simply fell in love with the place.

This new passion led to almost daily walks in every season in a voyage of discovery which included photography, painting, and

finally an all consuming interest in the natural and social history of the area.

I discovered that this wonderful piece of nature's engineering had changed the coastline and had a profound influence on all those who lived in the area. The Crumbles has seen it all. Soldiers, smugglers, a hospital, trains, planes, tragedies and happiness.

Much has changed in the last twenty years and before that, in each decade of the previous century. The surface of the Crumbles is largely hidden now but beneath it there still lies the great depth of closely packed pebbles – a sleeping giant protecting lowlying land from the sea.

This book, first published in 1996, is now in its third edition. It is the result of my love affair with an extraordinary example of maritime land and I hope the reader may enjoy a glimpse into its past.

Ann Botha
Langney Point, 2006

PART I - THE SOCIAL HISTORY
1. THE EARLY DAYS

There is one of the most wonderful views of the southern coastline of England from the eastern escarpment of the South Downs on the hills high above Eastbourne. The wide arc of Pevensey Bay leads the eye along the shore to the cliffs of Hastings and inland the flat green countryside of the old marshes are flanked many miles away, by low hills.

On a clear day it is possible to see the massive foreland of Dungeness low on the far horizon. Below lies Eastbourne, snug in the lea of Beachy Head, and the gentle curve of shore from the pier leads to Langney Point, southernmost tip of the shingle land of the Crumbles. Although formed in the same way as Dungeness,

the Crumbles is older in origin and comprises a shingle barrier that stretches from a point near the pier in Eastbourne along the coast to Normans Bay.

Two thousand years ago the coastline that we see today did not exist. A wide, shallow bay reached inland for some ten miles as far as Hailsham and Wartling. The sea covered all of the Willingdon and Pevensey levels, broken by a peninsula of land jutting out from the foot of the Downs. This great lagoon, dotted by islets and bordered by the rise of land to the north and east, must have been a beautiful and peaceful place.

At some time in the distant past a drift of pebbles settled on a bar of mud and sand at the entrance to the bay. The building of the Crumbles had begun. Fed by the sea with the drift of detritus of cliff and rock erosion a series of spits and islets of shingle began to join together to form a new shore.

The date of these early formations is unknown but when the Romans invaded Britain in the first century AD and during their occupation of four hundred years, the bay was still in existence, affording a sheltered harbour east of the great cliffs of Beachy Head.

Julius Caesar made early forays from Gaul to south east Britain in 55 and 54 BC, and one of these landings may have been in the area of Pevensey.

Before he withdrew his forces Caesar had overcome some of the powerful Celtic kingdoms in the south of Britain and made allies of others. Tributes of taxes established the first links between Britain and Rome. Nearly a hundred years later Claudius ordered the invasion of Britain and in AD 43 a large force sailed from Gaul. The resistance of the Britons who swept into battle in their chariots was overcome by the superior tactics and weaponry of the Romans. Within a few years the Claudian armies controlled the south as far as the river Severn. The tide of the conquerors swept north and the civilsation of Rome was imposed on Britain, combining with Celtic traditions and often using local lords in the system of government.

All of Britain as far as Hadrian's Wall bears the legacy of the long Roman occupation. In Eastbourne the remains of a Roman villa was found during excavations for the building of the promenade, its site near to the entrance of the present pier and built on what was then a small promontory of land overlooking the old bay. Britain prospered under the Romans and Christianity become one of the established religions. A continuing military presence was maintained to keep control and in the third century the Angles, Jutes and Saxons began to raid the coasts, posing a serious threat to south eastern areas.

The Romans built a series of strong stone forts along the line of defence, known as the Saxon Shore Forts. The largest of these nine forts was Anderita or Anderida, built at the end of the peninsula of land jutting out into the bay. The great Roman walls still stand as part of Pevensey Castle and can be clearly seen from the Crumbles across the flat fields that were once covered by the sea.

Anderita, which was built around 330 AD, was a massive structure, oval in shape to fit the contour of the peninsula. It was in a fine defensive position with a harbour on its northern side affording protection from the sea, and was the base for the Pevensey Fleet, *Classis Anderitianoram*, with a strong detachment of a crack unit of the British and Roman field army garrisoned within the walls.

The shore forts and defence forces were successful in repelling the Saxon raiders and for a century the south east was safe from attack. Then came the death knell to the years of peace. The Roman empire was failing and in the fifth century the Romans abandoned Britain.

In 477 the South Saxons, who gave Sussex its name, made their landing, probably near Chichester. Aelle, or Ella, the Saxon leader and his army were ruthless and hungry for land. The people of the south were powerless to stand against the invader's marches to the east and in 490 a great battle was fought on the peninsula for possession of the fort of Anderita.

The besieged defenders were supported by Britons attacking the

The coastline at Pevensey as it was in 340AD.

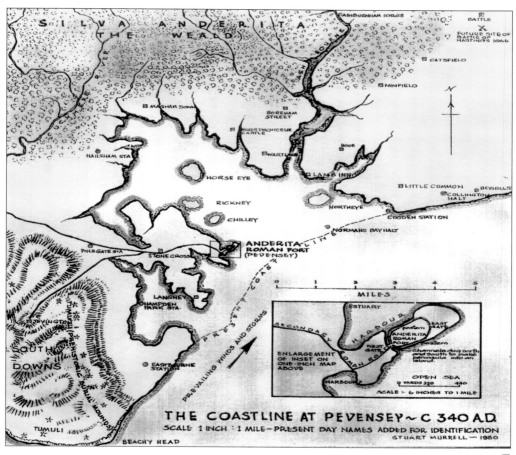

THE COASTLINE AT PEVENSEY ~ C 340 A.D.
SCALE 1 INCH : 1 MILE ~ PRESENT DAY NAMES ADDED FOR IDENTIFICATION
STUART MURRELL ~ 1980

Looking accross the Crumbles to Pevensey Castle.

Saxons from the nearby forest, but to no avail. The stronghold fell and according to the *Anglo Saxon Chronicles* Ella 'besieged the city of Andred and slew all that were therein, nor was one Briton left there afterwards'. This victory was an important one for Ella and led to his eventual domination of Sussex.

The Saxons left their mark on the place names in the area. The Saxon name for an islet was *ey* or *eye* and Langney, Pevensey, Northeye, Hydneye, Rickney and Horseye are reminders of the sites of islands or mounts of land in the former bay. The name of Pevensey is believed to derive from Ella's settlement outside the walls of the castle and comes from *Peofn*, a Saxon chieftan, and *eye*, island.

The Saxons held sway in southern England for many centuries. These were dark mysterious times with little recorded history. Those Britons who did not flee to the west were completely subjugated. Later the area was protected from incursions by the Danes by the impenetrable forests of Andreadsweald and by the eighth century had become part of the kingdom of Wessex.

Pevensey is mentioned as a port in 795 AD by Offa, who granted

The west wall of the Roman fort as it stands today.

its use to the Abbey of St Denys in France. Alfred the Great, King of Wessex in the ninth century, stemmed the Viking menace in the south east with a fleet of ships based in the Channel ports, one of which was Pevensey. The strategic position of this harbour continued to be of importance and accounts of the early eleventh century record Godwin and Harold sailing in and out of Pevensey with fleets of ships.

When the wide bay was still in existence, during this thousand years of history, it is possible that the shingle land of the Crumbles had begun to form. By the time of the Norman invasion of the eleventh century it may have stretched some way across the entrance to the bay, although the sea still reached far inland.

William, Duke of Normandy, set sail from France at the end of September in the year 1066 with a huge force of some 900 ships and 60,000 soldiers and cavalry, determined to stake his claim to the crown. No maps or documents now exist to indicate the formation of the coast at that time but the shore of the early Crumbles beaches would have been the nearest landing place in the vicinity of Pevensey.

John Speed's map of 1610 with the Crumbles shown as The Beach. Also clearly marked are the two small islets of shingle in the Romney estuary that formed the foundations of the foreland of Dungeness.

John Speed's map of 1610 shows this area as the scene of the invasion and, although it is not a true picture of the coastline at the time of William's incursion, the site of the landing is shown as the Crumbles. The inlet of Pevensey Haven had been forced eastwards by 1610 but in 1066 it would have met the sea further to the west. Within two weeks all of William's forces had landed and moved inland.

Harold and his army were engaged in the north in September of that fateful year, repelling invaders from Norway. Hastily rallying his army he made a forced march to the south and at the field of Senlac, some miles inland, he engaged the Normans in battle on the 14 October, 1066. Harold fell mortally wounded and William's army was victorious. The Normans were here to stay and William was crowned king in Westminster Abbey at the end of that year.

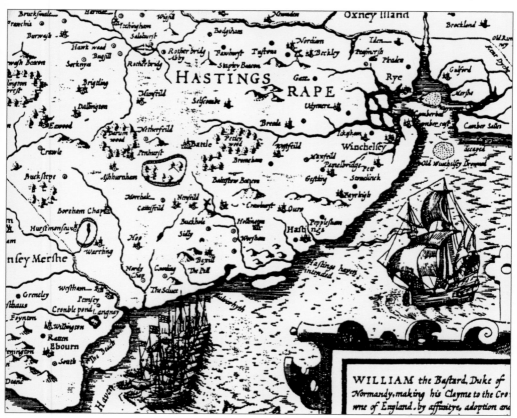

2. THE NEW LAND

After the Norman Conquest Robert of Mortain, half brother to William, became the feudal lord of Pevensey. This was the beginning of an era which saw the port grow and thrive and the castle became once again a powerful stronghold. The old Roman fortifications were strengthened and within the massive walls a Norman keep was built. Later great curtain walls, round towers and a gatehouse made Pevensey Castle an impregnable fortress. It was besieged four times in the following centuries and fell twice to famine, but never to direct assault.

The west walls, towers and moat of the Norman keep at Pevensey.

The first Norman church in England was built beyond the west gate of the castle in 1080 and another church erected outside the east gate in the early thirteenth century. St. Mary's in Westham and St. Nicholas in Pevensey stand today with part of their early Norman design intact. They are very old and very beautiful and, with the brooding majesty of Pevensey Castle nearby, continue to reflect the long past history of this ancient peninsula.

Corporation seal of Pevensey – Circa 1230 AD

In early Norman times it was still possible to sail boats into the bay at high tide as far as Hooe, Wartling and Herstmonceux. These villages became small ports, trading with boats going inland up the rivers and waterways. The rivers brought silt down from the countryside within so that the shores of the bay began to turn to marsh, a process encouraged by the weakening of tidal flows as the shingle bank of the Crumbles slowly encroached across the entrance to the bay.

Salt workings were established – for salt was essential in those days for the preservation of food – and the *Domesday* survey of 1080 reported a hundred salt works around the Pevensey marshes. The port, however, was still open to the sea, becoming one of the seven corporate members of the original Cinque ports.

This was a system introduced by Edward the Confessor for five ports in the south east to provide naval ships in return for self government. William continued the custom and the seal of Pevensey illustrates that often these naval ships were engagingly modest, being basically strong fishing boats with small wooden 'castles' or fighting platforms erected fore and aft.

The *Domesday Book* also mentions two holdings in 'Langlie' which were gifted to the priory in Lewes. This land was on a rise of ground some twenty feet above the marsh at the south west of Pevensey levels. It was built up by the monks and a chapel erected there in 1121. A part of it survives, incorporated into the later building of Langney Grange, c.1400.

When Lewes Priory was dissolved in 1537 the new

owners of the Langney holding used the property as a farm and for years it was known simply as Langney Farm. The house still stands much as it was when taken over in the sixteenth century and part of the building dates from the twelfth century. The lovely old building, now surrounded by modern housing, is still known as Langney Priory and until the late 1980s part of the old priory orchard remained at the foot of the slope bordered by the Langney streams.

Langney Priory, the house as it is today.

The first mention of the Crumbles was in documents dating from the days of the Normans, suggesting that by that time it was a well established area of land deserving of its own name. Documents relating to Pevensey Castle refer to a fisherman employed to take fish from the castle moat to *La Cromble*.

The Crumbles pond – now the lake in Princes Park, Eastbourne

13

*Langney Priory
Chapel*

– appears to have been used as a fish stew or stock pond because a further record, dated 1280, states that six men worked for a week emptying out the castle ditch from which seven casks of fish were taken to the pond *La Cromble*. This strangely evocative name has lasted to the present day and is believed to derive from the Old English word *Cruma*, meaning a morsel, or fragment or crumb, perhaps denoting the nature of the pebbly ground.

During the three centuries after the Norman invasion a rich and colourful life evolved in and around Pevensey and the castle. The stronghold passed into the hands of many notables including the Aquila family, who built Michelham Priory, the Earl of Pembroke, Peter de Savoy, whose land in London gave his name to the Savoy Hotel, Queen Margaret, wife of Edward II, and John of Gaunt, Duke of Lancaster.

Princes and kings with their knights and retainers on state business were entertained at the castle with hunting and tournaments. A feudal court was held every three weeks at the West Gate and the port was busy with embarkations and arrivals of dignitaries and ships of trade and naval defence.

While Pevensey port and the castle enjoyed their times of power, what was later to become the town of Eastbourne consisted of two small hamlets. On the hill leading to the top of the Downs a Norman church was built and the Lamb Inn, which still exists, also dates from the thirteenth century. The name of Beachy Head is thought to date back to Norman times, derived from the French *Beau Chef*, meaning beautiful headland.

Nature, sublimely indifferent to the affairs of men, was taking its own course. The early shingle ridges of the Crumbles land that were already in existence in Norman times, began to increase dramatically some 800 years ago and gradually the sea was cut off from the old embayment.

Pevensey became a port connected to the sea by a river, then this too silted up with gravel and mud. Strenuous efforts were made to keep the outlet open but to no avail. The old port was doomed.

As the sea receded Pevensey lost its defensive importance and the castle fell into disrepair. The Crown could not afford the cost of maintenance and by the sixteenth century the stronghold was deserted. Everything, it seemed, had changed. By the early 1600's the Crumbles had become a vast beachland, extending out to sea for nearly two miles at its widest part and reaching along the coast from Eastbourne to Normans Bay near the village of Cooden.

During the Middle Ages work began in the task of reclaiming the marshy bay from the sea. Labourers built earthen walls known as innings and moved them steadily forward. They were often hampered by storms and flooding, in particular a great storm of 1287 and by further sea flooding some 200 years later. Finally the work was completed – a wonderful feat of manual engineering and sheer hard work, aided by the barrier of the Crumbles as it built up along the shore.

Although the formation of the great beach meant the end of Pevensey as a port it enabled the establishment of a new coastal countryside and to this day the Crumbles continues to protect the levels and the lowlying lands of Eastbourne from the sea.

3. A LONELY PLACE

In medieval times the French became a threat to the south coast of England and for many years their raids caused damage and loss of life. The Crumbles was the scene of such a raid when fifteen French galleys landed at Eastbourne in the fourteenth century.

Here was a great beach with a shallow shore where invasion from the sea was cause for concern. In the reign of Elizabeth I it was clear that the Spanish were assembling an Armada of great strength for an assault upon England and a survey was made of the coast of Sussex in 1587 to prepare urgent defences.

A map made at this time shows the Crumbles in great detail and the survey states of the area. 'Is all alongste good landings upon the Beache, but they cannot entre into the Lande partely for Marshes, partely for marshe and high land together... but must of necessity march alongst the sea except... at the haven mouth of K and L'. Fortunately there was no attempt to land when the Spanish Armada sailed up the Channel in 1588. It passed Sussex without firing a shot on the coast.

The lowlying beaches and river mouths of the south coast were vulnerable to other marauders. Smuggling was rife from the fourteenth century when an onerous duty of fifty shillings a sack was levied on wool growers. Huge flocks of sheep were kept in Sussex and wool was smuggled out of the country to avoid the heavy duty. The smugglers were known as owlers as their operations took place at night. Their activities grew to tremendous proportions and on their return trips goods including silk, lace, tobacco, tea and spirits were smuggled into the country.

The two way traffic in illicit trade reached its height in the seventeenth and eighteenth centuries. It was known as 'free trade' and tolerated and accepted by the local population. Many people were part of it in one way or another, either by buying the goods or helping with the smuggling. Fishermen and farm labourers often enjoyed a secondary job as lookouts or in helping to unload the boats on the beaches.

A small number of customs officers and their few armed men were often powerless to stop the smuggling gangs which ranged from a few men with a boat to large and well organised groups of free traders.

The Crumbles was a fine and lonely place for nocturnal landings and there are many recorded incidents. In 1733 an officer saw 'tracks of men and horses on the Sea Beach' and together with other customs officers and two Dragoons followed the men to Wilmington where the group were stopped and searched and the booty of tea and coffee seized.

In 1744 the forces of law were not so successful. Customs officers and a small force of Dragoons were sent to Pevensey where a large band of about one hundred men were bringing in spirits. However, the forces of the revenue were hopelessly outnumbered. The shouts and clash of steel echoed far along the beach on that dark night and the customs men and Dragoons had to beat a hasty retreat leaving the smugglers to unload their cargo of contraband and make off to London.

During the often turbulent reigns of the Tudors and Stuarts this small corner of south east England remained relatively quiet and remote from the affairs of the powerful but inevitably the tide turned – almost literally for the Crumbles for the deposits of shingle which had drifted in for many long years were now depleted. The fickle sea began to erode and carry away a part of its original gift. The curved shore and the foreland of Langney Point came into being in the 1700s, although the shoreline was then much further out than it is today.

In 1714 the House of Hanover came to the throne of England and a new era began. At that time four small hamlets to the west of the Crumbles formed the nucleus of the town later to become Eastbourne. These were Bourne, Meads and Southbourne together with the fishing fraternity at the shore in a small community known as Sea Houses. The health giving properties of mineral water, spa water, and best of all sea water, were extolled by the medical men of the day and by 1760 sea bathing had become fashionable and visitors came to Sea Houses near the western edge of the vast Crumbles beach.

After George III's children were sent there for a holiday in 1780 there were improvements made for the visitors and by the early nineteenth century Eastbourne was referred to as 'a popular place for families of distinction'.

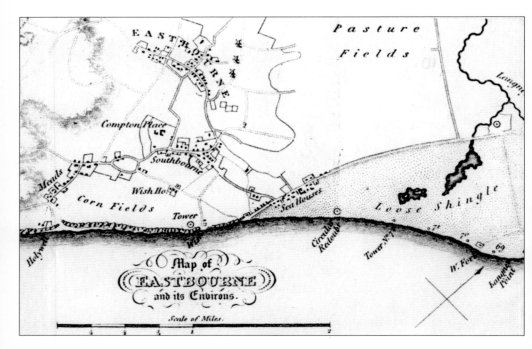

Map of 1819, with the Martello towers marked, and the pond on the Crumbles.

At this time the Crumbles was to see its first buildings. Since 1798 Napoleon Bonaparte had been preparing to invade the south coast of England and between 1803 and 1805 a force of 130,000 men and more than 2,000 ships were marshalled at Boulougne. To combat the threat British troops were stationed in the south and a letter written from Eastbourne in October 1803 said 'everything here is on the alert to receive the enemy'.

As early as 1795 a small fort was built near Langney Point, known as East Langney fort, and gun emplacements were constructed along the shore line. Eastbourne soon became a garrison town and a newspaper of the 1803 reported: 'the whole of the 11th Light Dragoons have been ordered from their different outposts… and are encamped between South Bourne and Pevensey'. Also: 'Three regiments of regulars are hourly expected to occupy the spacious barracks erected on the Shingles' – the site of the present day Territorial Army building in Seaside.

Meanwhile the government decided that strong towers should be built along the coastline, the design based on a tower at Mortalla Point in Corsica, which had withstood a fierce onslaught by the

British in 1793. More than a hundred of what came to be known as Martello towers were built along the south and east coasts. Fourteen were erected between Beachy Head and Pevensey of which twelve were on the shoreline of the Crumbles and one on St. Anthony's Mount, a rise of land about a mile inland from Langney Point. The remaining tower – the Wish Tower – was built in Eastbourne on a rise of ground.

The Grenadier and Scots Guards at ease inside the Redoudt. Photo: Eastbourne Herald

A large circular fortress called the Redoubt was also built on the Crumbles, nearer to the town; and another small fort was erected west of the Point.

Work began on the Martello towers in 1805 and by 1808 all the ones at Eastbourne and along the shore of the Crumbles were completed. They were built to a high standard of craftsmanship by John Smith of Eastbourne, supervised by the Royal Engineers. The walls on the seaward side were thirteen feet thick and some six feet thick on the inland side; the height being thirty three feet. In each tower roughly half a million bricks were used, enough to build fifty three-bedroomed houses today. They were circular in shape, the base measuring forty eight feet across, decreasing to forty feet at the top.

On the flat roof was a twenty four pounder gun mounted on a carriage so it could traverse in a full circle. The towers had two windows and a door twenty feet from the ground, facing inland and reached by a wooden ladder. Inside were two floors and a staircase built into the thickness of the walls. A strong central pillar supported the roof and the heavy gun and the ceilings inside arched and vaulted with perfectly dovetailed brickwork. The estimated cost of each was about £3,000 but the actual cost was probably higher.

After the Battle of Trafalgar in 1805 when Nelson defeated the French and Spanish fleets the threat of invasion by Napoleon receded and the British victory at Waterloo in 1815 ensured that all fears of the French were gone. This led to accusations that the defences of the south and east coasts had been a waste of public money but there is no doubt that if invasion had taken place the Martello towers would have proved their worth.

In any event the towers and forts on the Crumbles were used by garrisons of soldiers for many years, each accommodating an officer and twenty four men. The Redoubt, too, was in use for more than fifty years. It was imaginatively designed, strongly built, boasted twelve pieces of cannon mounted on the flat roof that encircled the inner courtyard and was capable of housing 350 men together with provisions for several weeks.

The Redoubt still stands on Eastbourne seafront in an excellent state of preservation. The warren of rooms were used for some years as a museum of the history of the Sussex regiments and until the end of summer 2005, band concerts were a feature, often ending with the very apt 1812 overture.

When the towers and forts were first built roadways led across the Crumbles from the tower on St. Anthony's Mount to the East and West Langney forts on the shore. These roads were known as northways, eventually becoming 'Nor'ways'. The name of Norway was given to a hamlet on the northern boundary of the Crumbles near to the junction of Seaside and Lottbridge Drove.

The name of Seaside seems confusing to the visitor today as it is not by the sea, but in the early nineteenth century it was the main toll road east to Pevensey, bordered on the south only by the shingle beach of the Crumbles.

Many of the Martello towers of Eastbourne fell prey to the sea. Gone too are the gun emplacements and the forts of East and West Langney. The erosion of the Crumbles continued and Tower No. 65 was split apart by rough seas in 1935. Some of the towers that were being undermined by the sea were used for gunnery practice in the nineteenth century and their strength was demonstrated when No. 71 was bombarded for two days but even then considered capable of repair.

Where Tower 65 and East Langney fort once stood the sea now meets the entrance to the Sovereign Harbour and only six Martellos remain between Eastbourne and Pevensey.

A turn of the century picture of the Martello towers taken from the East Langney fort.

Coal empties returning from the gas works along the Ballast Line.

The crossing keeper's cottage, Seaside, in 1964.

4. THE CRUMBLES RAILWAY

After the Napoleonic wars the nation's economy took some time to recover and the four small residential areas comprising Eastbourne at that time stayed much the same for some years. Visitors still came to the town for sea bathing in the summer months but generally it was a quiet place, the journey to London by horse-drawn coach taking nine hours.

The arrival of the railway encouraged further development. In 1849 a branch line was built across the Willingdon levels to Eastbourne providing transport for passengers and goods and bringing in a faster pace of life.

The great shingle bank of the Crumbles played its own part in the growth of the town and was also for many years a source of ballast that was essential to the new railway networks. In 1857 and 1862 the London Brighton and South East Railway negotiated agreements with the Duke of Devonshire, owner of the Crumbles, for the company to purchase not less than 48,000 cubic yards of shingle per year at a price of one penny per cubic yard.

To reach the beachland a small branch railway was built and continued in use for some seventy years to the Crumbles and for a further thirty years to serve industrial sidings. It was known as the Ballast Line, or simply as the Crumbles Railway and its track was seven yards wide and nearly three and a half miles long. It left the main line near Eastbourne Station and, when first built, ran through open countryside, crossing the turnpike road, now Seaside, at a point not far from the Lottbridge cattle drove, which was then a rough track leading to Willingdon.

At the crossing there was a keeper's cottage, a building of white weatherboard with a tiled roof. The engine drivers' working instructions advised that: 'Great care must be exercised in crossing the turnpike road to and from the Ballast Hole' and they must 'keep a good lookout for road traffic, and the engine whistle must be sounded on approaching the road'. The line continued on the Crumbles eastwards for another one and a half miles to the Ballast Hole.

Every day the small steam trains chugged to and fro between Eastbourne Station and the Crumbles wharves. Thousands of tons of shingle were used each year as ballast for the railways until in the 1920s the increasing speed of trains necessitated a change and Meldon granite chippings replaced the old beach ballast.

In addition to its use as railway ballast the shingle was also taken to the Duke of Devonshire's depots near Eastbourne Station for building purposes and this traffic continued until 1931. After that the shingle beds were leased to Hall and Company, a large building firm who installed a mechanical plant to grade the gravel into varying sizes. An extensive two foot gauge railway was laid for small but powerful Simplex tractors to haul the shingle to the plant on the northern borders of the Crumbles. The firm had its own lorries for transport so the standard gauge railway was needed no longer. All rail traffic over the level crossing at Seaside, which had become a busy road, ceased by 1932.

During its long and busy life the Ballast Line had sidings which connected with the gas works, built in 1870 near Lottbridge Drove, and the old waterworks. A timber yard, brickworks and later depots of British Petroleum and the electricity works also had sidings connected to the Crumbles Railway. So the small line became important to the fast growing town, a means of transport for more than shingle; even conveying loads of fertiliser to farms adjoining the tracks.

It was an ordered, slow and friendly little railway, where the drivers knew everyone and allowed small boys to hitch a ride to school in the mornings. Occasionally the Crumbles railway had a glamorous visitor. The flat landscape provided an ideal location for official photographs so to the beachland were brought the gleaming brilliance of the latest rolling stock, including the Southern Belle Pullman of 1908. It made a magnificent picture before going into service between London and Brighton.

After the crossing in Seaside was closed the line continued to serve various industrial sidings and conveyed thousands of tons of coal to the gas works. Two small sturdy little engines named Mary and Anne were used by the Gas Company on their extensive sidings. Sadly these became redundant when the Crumbles railway and its sidings were finally closed in 1966 and although they were advertised for sale in 1967 in *The Railway Magazine* no acceptable offers were received. They were therefore cut up in 1968.

Anne and Mary at the gas works. These small engines were built by the Avonside Company of Bristol. Photo: S.G. Nash.

The age of the steam trains continues to hold a fascination for people everywhere. Noisy, dirty, puffing out clouds of smoke the locomotives may be but they had style and a sense of power about them that was hard to resist. Now all of the tracks of the old Ballast Line have been removed. Its existence enabled the shingle from the Crumbles to become literally a part of the town as it was used in the construction of new residential areas at the centre and eventually on the western end of the Crumbles itself.

5. THE LANDOWNER

The man who was to exert his interest and influence in the early planning of Eastbourne was William Cavendish, the seventh Duke of Devonshire, owner of the Crumbles, the sea frontage and extensive areas at the centre of the growing town. He was a grandson of the first Earl of Burlington, who married Lady Elizabeth Compton in 1782, and he inherited his grandfather's estates in 1834 when he was twenty six years old.

In 1858 a further inheritance bestowed upon him huge estates and the title of seventh Duke of Devonshire. Besides the Sussex properties which had accrued to him earlier there were lands and estates in England and Ireland, including the magnificent Chatsworth House in Derbyshire. The family had originally come from the Suffolk village of Cavendish, rising to power and wealth by favour of kings and politicians. The male line also followed the popular principle of the aristocracy by marrying well, thus adding to the family fortunes.

By the nineteenth century the estates and possessions of the family reached vast proportions. However, the seventh Duke of Devonshire was by all accounts, a man who had no taste for the glittering social scene. He was a scholar with a brilliant mind, who had taken a First in classics and mathematics at Cambridge. This quiet, clever, strongly religious man had a great sense of duty towards managing his many estates.

Although he showed interest in the early development of Eastbourne this waned when his wife died at a tragically early age in the 1840s. Later however, this interest revived and he was

This statue of William Cavendish, seventh Duke of Devonshire, the man who made Eastbourne, gazes thoughtfully out to sea from the top of Devonshire Place.

influential in persuading the railway company to open the branch line to the town.

With its arrival development began in earnest. Well planned wide streets lined with trees were laid out and large comfortable houses built. Overseen by the Duke's agents and working in collaboration with the local authorities and the Gilbert family who owned and developed the northern areas of the town, Eastbourne was soon established as a model of the respectable Victorian resort and a favoured place for families of quality to reside in or visit. Promenades were built on the low cliffs to Holywell and along the shore to the Redoubt.

As in all successful ventures a happy combination of the right time and the right man coincided to create a thriving town. Britain's population grew from eight million in 1801 to nearly eighteen million in 1851. A middle class emerged, drawn from people in professions and in trade, with money and time for leisure. Many towns and villages benefited and grew in the wake of a national obsession with the sea, and Eastbourne became a popular resort.

The seventh Dukes was held in great esteem for the part he played and was generous with his backing, often making outright gifts to the town. All this spending was not entirely philanthropic as with a business venture on the grand scale it was in the Duke's interest to ensure that growth continued.

When development first began in Eastbourne there was only the small hamlet of Norway on the Crumbles, which included Vine Square, Norway Cottages, the Archery tavern and the Lodge Inn. In 1859 the building of Christ Church was completed. Its parish boundaries included Rowes land, an agricultural area later known as Roselands. The fishermen and their boats were moved from their old site at Sea Houses to the beaches east of the Redoubt and Christ Church became known as the Fishermens Church.

In the 1860s residential building began on the western end of the Crumbles. The shingle land between the shore and the old turnpike road gradually filled with streets of well built but modest housing to accommodate the families of the artisans and those who provided services to the fashionable centre. The estate eventually reached the site of the old Crumbles pond and there for the time being, the building stopped.

The later half of the nineteenth century saw other uses for the beachland. The first sewage outfall for the town was opened at Langney Point in 1867 and in 1895/7 this was improved and a new cast iron outfall constructed on the same site.

The opening of the first outfall in 1867 was a grand and formal occasion and on the great day all the shops in the town closed early. The streets were lined with flags and bunting and a large crowd followed a procession of seventy carriages and a band to Langney Point. On arrival at the outfall the works were formally opened by the Duke and, with a bottle of wine, he christened it the Devonshire outfall. An illuminated address was read out, couched in flowery and fulsome praise of the Duke, and it was received with deafening cheers from the crowd.

The Crumbles and the hamlet of Norway, 1888. Photo: Towner Art Gallery.

That night a formal dinner at which the Duke was guest of honour, was held at the Anchor Hotel. It was an occasion typical of the times with local officials expressing adulation to their benefactor for all he had done for Eastbourne – no doubt with a keen eye to future support and financial backing.

In 1895 Langney Point became again the site for a building which needed to be far from the town it served. In the days before the use of vaccination the diseases of smallpox, scarlet fever, diptheria and enteric fever were serious threats and the only effective way of checking infection was to isolate the infected patients. Langney Hospital, built in 1895/6, was situated just east of Langney Point and close to the shore. It cost £1,250, had eighteen beds and was sometimes known as the Smallpox

The isolation hospital east of Langney Point. Photo: Eastbourne Library.

Hospital. From the records it appears that all the patients recovered, secure in the homely atmosphere and surrounded by plenty of sea breezes. The hospital was eventually closed in 1940 and demolished after World War II.

The spectacular growth of Eastbourne at this time is reflected in the population figures, which were 1,668 in 1801, rising to 34,278 in 1891. By 1901 the figure had reached 43,337 and today it is some 92,000, the town having spread both to the north and east.

In 1901 Kings Drive was built along what had once been part of the shoreline of the old bay of Roman times. This road gave access to the new Hampden Park, a pleasure ground laid out on the site of the Ham Shaw woods and the Decoy pond. Around the park a new residential area was built, becoming part of the borough of Eastbourne. This was another boundary of the shoreline of the ancient bay and in Roman times Hampden Park station on the edge of the Willingdon levels would have been under two metres of water.

In 1891 the seventh Duke of Devonshire died and was succeeded by his son, Spencer Compton. He was more socially inclined than his retiring father and became mayor for a year, as did the ninth Duke, Victor Cavendish. However, with the passing of the seventh Duke the flow of finance from the family into the town gradually ceased in favour of other interests and they no longer lived in Eastbourne.

....

6. WINGS AND THINGS

In 1911 two remarkable men joined forces to form the **Eastbourne Aviation Company. The Crumbles, having shared in a modest way the coming of age of the train, now saw some of the first aeroplanes.**

Frederick Bernard Fowler and Frank Hucks were larger than life characters with a taste for adventure that made them ideal candidates to both fly and build aeroplanes.

Fowler had served an engineering apprenticeship and apparently taught himself to fly, soon obtaining his pilot's certificate. He bought fifty acres of land in the south east corner of the Willingdon levels behind St. Anthony's hill, had the drainage ditches boarded over to give an airstrip of some 560 yards and built two large sheds.

There in 1911, with Victor Yates as his partner, he opened the Eastbourne Flying School. It had two Bleriot monoplanes and seven more small planes were purchased from a flying school in Beaulieu, Hampshire.

For £30 a person could learn to fly, although this tuition fee later rose to £90. Pleasure flights were available for two guineas and these were very popular. A designer was taken on to build new monoplanes and pupils, including several naval men, were taught to fly on Bleriot monoplanes and a Bristol biplane. The Langney aerodrome was up and running.

Major F.B. Fowler. Photo: Towner Art Gallery.

Members of the Eastbourne Aviation Company pose for photographs in front of the seaplane sheds. Photo: Towner Art Gallery.

Meanwhile Frank Hucks, one of the first seaplane pilots in Britain, was touring seaside resorts giving passenger flights and flying displays. He had formed the Frank Hucks Waterplane Company with C.W. von Roemer of Herstmonceux and it used two Henry Farman floatplanes. On a visit to Eastbourne Frank Hucks met F.B. Fowler and together they formed the Eastbourne Aviation Company.

A hangar was erected on the Crumbles to the east of the present day Sovereign Centre. A rail track and turntable were laid across the shingle to the sea and used to launch seaplanes at high tide. Soon two more hangars were built and what was known for many years as the Seaplane Sheds became a busy and active part of the Crumbles shore.

Many planes were made there, including Bleriot monoplanes, Henry Farman biplanes, Avro 504 models and a successful monoplane designed by a Mr. Gassler for the company in 1913. The flying school and aerodrome on the levels and the aircraft factory about a mile south on the Crumbles became a successful combination, the company participating in exhibition flights and aero shows in Britain and abroad.

At the outbreak of war with Germany in 1914 the factory was expanded as orders for seaplanes were received from the Admiralty and the Langney aerodrome was requisitioned and enlarged for the training of Royal Naval Air Service pilots.

F.B. Fowler became a temporary Flight Lietenant and by the end of the war years had risen to the rank of Major. Frank Hucks joined the Navy in the engineering branch. By October, 1915, Eastbourne had become an important Royal Naval Air Service flying school with nearly thirty different types of small planes used for instruction.

The aircraft factory was soon busy with orders from the Admiralty for seaplanes and later for repair work. There were also orders from the War Office for Avro aircraft – light single-engined bi-planes, produced at a cost of about £4,400 each. In 1915 C.E. Mayo was made a director of the company and the following year the registered office was transferred to the factory on the Crumbles.

At the end of the war in 1918 Major Fowler re-activated the flying school and restarted the popular joy rides from the

An Avro seaplane fitted with a 130hp Clerget engine, at the end of the launching runway. Photo: Towner Art Gallery.

Flying machines always attracted the crowds. Here onlookers have gathered to watch the launch of a Gnome rotary engined seaplane.

aerodrome. For a while business was good and the Crumbles factory, now that the government contracts had come to an end, was used for the construction of Avro sea-planes.

Sadly, however, the days of the Aviation Company's prosperity came to an end and in spite of Major Fowler's efforts to keep things going by organising races and flying displays, public interest gradually waned. The aerodrome licence was cancelled at the end of 1920 because of the heavy expense of maintaining the landing strip and when the Air Ministry decided not to retain Langney as a supplementary landing ground it was closed completely, reverting to its original state as farm land.

The seaplane business also foundered and the company tried to find other uses for the sheds on the Crumbles. Attempts were made to market a small light motor car and to construct charabanc bodies, but these ventures failed. By the end of 1922 the bank appointed a receiver and the workforce was reduced to a minimum.

Although the Eastbourne Aviation Company was not finally dissolved until 1932 work ceased in the Crumbles factory in 1924.

Jim Mollinson's Gypsy Moth, surrounded by spectators, after bad weather forced him to land on the Crumbles. Photo: E. Tompsett.

The sheds were sold to Eastbourne Corporation in 1926 and stood virtually unused for years before being demolished in 1940. A sad end to a once thriving business but while it lasted the company proved its worth in peacetime pleasure and fulfilled a valuable role in the war years of 1914-18.

Seven years after the seaplane sheds closed the Crumbles had an unexpected visitor. On 6 August 1931 the sound of a small aircraft engine was heard, approaching from the sea. It was Jim Mollison, the famous aviator, on the last leg of a record breaking flight from Australia to England in his Gipsy Moth plane.

Encountering bad weather over the Channel he flew in low to the coast and seeing what appeared to be an expanse of flat land covered by waving grass he made a forced landing on the Crumbles. A bumpy one too, as the shingle which had been hidden from sight in the air was far from ideal for a landing and the small plane nearly pitched forward on its nose. A small crowd of excited onlookers helped drag the plane to firmer ground near the Pevensey Bay Road and when the weather improved Jim Mollison took off for Croydon to set a new Australia to England flight record of eight days, twenty two hours, thirty five minutes.

Many years later two other aircraft were not so lucky as the tiny Gipsy Moth. In 1955 a Sunderland flying boat crashed and broke up on the beach near Langney Point and in 1989 a light aircraft met the same fate. People on the beaches rushed to the aid of the two men in the crashed plane, but although injured and shocked they survived and were taken to the Eastbourne hospital where they made a full recovery.

In 1931 another piece of aviation history was also seen at Eastbourne. On 18 August the great airship, the Graf Zeppelin, passed over the Crumbles at a low altitude on her way to Hanworth. It was huge – 775 feet long and 100 feet wide. Onlookers said its progress was slow but it was probably travelling at about 65 – 70mph and took three minutes to reach Beachy Head before disappearing from view.

The Graf Zeppelin flying over the Crumbles in 1931. Photo: S.C. Nash.

7. THE CRUMBLES MURDERS

When aviation was in its infancy the Crumbles had seen another page of history unfold but it had also been the scene of two sensational murders.

The violent deaths of two young women achieved great notoriety at the time and even today Eastbourne is haunted by these events, the first of which was a tragic example of the wisdom of the old adage 'never talk to strangers'.

Irene Munro, pictured below, was a dark haired and attractive girl of seventeen who lived in London with her widowed mother and worked as a shorthand typist in Oxford Street.

In August of 1920 her mother went to visit relatives in Scotland and agreed that Irene, who was an independent girl, could have a holiday on her own at the seaside.

Irene Munro

Irene looked older than her years, often being taken for twenty or even twenty five. She had been on holiday alone the previous year at Brighton, where she was born. This year she picked Eastbourne and with the casualness of the very young set off early from London with no accommodation booked in advance.

It was the height of the holiday season and lodgings were hard to find, but in the late afternoon Irene Munro found a room to let at 393 Seaside. The landlady, a Mrs. Wynniatt, said she could have the room at thirty shillings a week from the following day and for that night she could stay at a neighbour's house at

Norman Cottages in Wartling Road. All was set for what promised to be an enjoyable holiday.

The next morning Irene walked down to the beach across the Crumbles. A young naval stoker, William Putland, who was home on leave in Eastbourne was on the beach, one of a crowd watching a seaplane take up passengers. Putland noticed a girl sitting nearby wearing a green velour coat. The vivid colour impressed itself on his mind and when he saw it again on two later occasions he was sure that it was the same girl. William Putland was to become an important witness to later events.

On the morning of Thursday, 19 August, Irene wrote to her mother telling of a walk to Beachy Head. On the previous day she told her landlady she had walked to Pevensey and also made a trip into town. Mrs. Wynniatt had the impression that Irene Munro was a pretty and happy young girl, respectable and sensible. Not, alas, sensible enough as it turned out. For on the afternoon of 19 August Irene left her lodgings for a walk, returning after a few minutes to fetch her coat, the green velour. A painter working nearby looked down and saw the girl walking along with two men. All three walked away in the direction of the Crumbles, a walk from which Irene Munro was never to return.

That night Mrs. Wynniatt stayed up till midnight but there was no sign of her young lodger and she did not return on the following day. The landlady decided Irene must have gone to visit her relatives in Brighton but by Saturday she was feeling more concerned and when her husband saw in the local paper that a woman's body had been found on the Crumbles on the previous day the worried couple went to the police to report their visitor's absence. They were taken to the mortuary where they were horrified to be shown the body of Irene. Her face was badly disfigured by a violent attack but the clothes were unmistakable, especially the green coat.

On Friday afternoon, 20 August, a Mrs. Weller and her thirteen year old son, William, had gone for a walk and a picnic on the Crumbles. William wandered off and running into a small hollow in the shingle he tripped on something and saw to his horror that it was the foot of a woman. Rushing back to his mother he told her what he had seen and they returned to their lodgings.

Their landlady's husband, a Mr. Lamb, went back with William and pushed away the shingle to reveal the body of Irene Munro. The boy was sent to fetch the police who found a heavy ironstone brick nearby on which there were bloodstains. More police arrived and a doctor who decided death had occurred some twenty four hours previously. The body was taken to the mortuary and Irene's mother and aunt were contacted and travelled to Eastbourne at the weekend for the awful duty of formal identification.

Scotland Yard were called in and on Saturday, 21 August a Chief Inspector Mercer arrived and visited the scene of the crime. Five men who had been at the ballast workings on the day of the murder told the inspector they had seen two men and a girl walking along the tracks. One of the men had his arm round the girl's waist and all three seemed 'jolly and laughing'. They had walked on in the direction of Pevensey, the man with the girl carrying a stick.

The labourers were asked to go to the mortuary and all five identified Irene Munro as the girl they had seen. A post mortem examination indicated that a blow had been struck on the face, probably with a stick, producing unconsciousness, the heavy ironstone brick completing the fatal injury. There were no signs of any other assault. All the details were reported in the press and Eastbourne hummed with rumour and speculation.

Now the hunt was on and the trail led inexorably to two young men, both residents of Eastbourne – William Thomas Gray and Jack Alfred Field. On 24 August they were arrested and interviewed by the police. Gray was twenty eight and married to a local girl. Field was a younger man of twenty, discharged from the Navy and had previously been in trouble with the police. Both were out of work and constantly together, sharing a liking for bars and the cinemas and casual flirtations. Where they got the money for this easy life nobody knew.

Witnesses came forward linking the two men with Irene Munro and when interviewed by the police both Field and Gray told roughly the same story, saying they had spent Thursday together, meeting a friend called Maud at Pevensey Castle.

They denied knowing Irene Munro or going on the Crumbles, Gray saying that 'he had never been there in his life'. Suspicion of the pair remained, although the railway labourers were unable to pick out either man at an identification parade. Their friend,

Maud, flatly denied meeting them at Pevensey on the Thursday afternoon that the murder took place as all that day she was in the house where she was employed as a servant. This fact was corroborated by her fellow workers.

On 26 August Field and Gray were released but the police now found more witnesses who had seen the two together on the day of Irene's death, including the young naval stoker, William Putland, with the young girl's brilliant green coat providing a strong clue. Field and Gray were arrested again and charged with the murder on 4 September. Two days later the adjourned inquest resumed and gave a verdict of 'wilful murder'. Both men pleaded not guilty and were committed for trial at the next assizes.

On 13 December, 1920, their trial began at the County Hall, Lewes, before Mr. Justice Avory and lasted for five days.

Counsel for the Crown prosecution included Mr. Curtis Bennett KC and Mr. C.F. Gill KC. Field was defended by Mr. J.D. Cassels and Mr. G.P. Robinson, Gray by Sir Edward Marshall Hall, KC and Mr. John Flowers. These were all illustrious names in the courts of the time and an indication of the sensational aspects of the case. The defence were financed by the magazine *John Bull*.

The case for the prosecution was based on circumstantial evidence. No-one had seen the crime committed and both the accused continued to plead not guilty but a stream of witnesses were called to give evidence. The brilliant Marshall Hall made the point that many of the witnesses were uncertain as to the description and colour of clothes, but the tide was turning against Field and Gray. Before being charged with the murder both had attempted to join the army. They had concocted the alibi concerning Maud Baxter and more damningly Gray had tried to persuade another inmate while in Maidstone Prison awaiting trial, to help him establish another alibi for 19 August.

Field was the only witness for the defence. He denied much of the evidence already heard but acknowledged that he and Gray had agreed together to say Maud Baxter had been with them at Pevensey. He said they knew they could not prove where they were. Shown a walking stick he admitted it was one that belonged to his father but said he had not used it for at least a fortnight before the murder. Gray did not give evidence.

In his summing up, Mr. Justice Avory said that there was no

doubt that Irene Munro had been murdered. The joint charge meant that the men were acting together and it was immaterial which man had actually committed the violence. Dealing with the question of motive the judge said it could have been robbery or to combat resistance to an attempted assault.

The jury retired at four minutes past two and returned an hour later with a guilty verdict for both men but with a recommendation for mercy on the grounds that they believed the crime was not premeditated. Neither of the accused had anything to say in mitigation and formal sentence of death was passed by the judge.

This was not quite the end of the dreadful story. An appeal was heard in January, 1921, before the Lord Chief Justice and two other judges. Both Field and Gray spoke on their own behalf, each man saying that the other had confessed to the crime, each man also saying that they had not been there at the scene. These further statements conflicted once more with their own previous statements and that of witnesses. The appeal was dismissed.

At Wandsworth Prison on 4 February, 1921, Field and Gray met their death by hanging.

No on will ever know what actually happened on that hot Thursday afternoon so long ago. Neither Field or Gray gave themselves the relief of true confession but only tried to implicate the other. Irene Munro had been foolish as only the young can be, to go for a walk in a lonely place with two men. Did a flirtatious episode get out of hand? Perhaps.

The sad and awful consequence of that walk was that three people, once 'jolly and laughing' all lost their lives.

The Officer's House – scene of the murder of Emily Kaye. The bungalow was demolished in 1953.

A second murder took place on the Crumbles in 1924 and was known for years afterwards as 'The Bungalow Murder'. A few cottages, once occupied by coastguards, stood isolated on the beachland at the border of Eastbourne and Pevensey. One, called the Officer's House, was a neat whitewashed building and in the spring of 1924 was leased for two months at a rent of three and a half guineas a week to Patrick Herbert Mahon, a man of thirty four, using the name of Waller.

Mahon had taken on the bungalow ostensibly as a romantic hideaway for himself and his mistress, Emily Kaye, and on 7 April 1924 Emily travelled to Eastbourne and moved into the bungalow believing that this was the start of a new life with her lover.

Oddly enough she was also a shorthand typist but unlike Irene Munro she was not a foolish young girl but a woman of thirty seven, tall, fair-haired and coolly attractive. A thoroughly nice person according to a cousin who said 'a better girl never lived'.

However, the warning bells had not rung for Irene Munro and they did not ring for Emily Kaye. She worked for a firm of accountants in London and had met Patrick Mahon who often called at her office and soon began an affair with him. She knew he was married but believed he would leave his wife and that they would start a new life together. She also knew by chance that

Mahon had previously been in prison for a bank raid but she was pregnant and very much in love with the dark good-looking Irishman. She readily agreed to leave her job and embark on the venture he proposed.

Unfortunately for Emily she did not know that Patrick Mahon was an indefatigable and practised womaniser with an unsavoury past which included fraud as well as the bank raid which had landed him in prison for five years.

He had married a young Irish girl when he was twenty one, and his wife, Mavourneen, had stood by him when he was imprisoned. Now Mahon was involved with a woman who did not take the affair lightly, who was pregnant, and who expected him to leave his wife. He was in a fix.

Having installed Emily in the Crumbles cottage Mahon continued to go home to his wife most days during the week. True to form he struck up a new acquaintance with a young woman at Richmond, an Ethel Duncan. Never one to miss another romantic interlude he arranged to take her out to dinner the following week.

Emily Kaye.
Photo: Eastbourne
Gazette

On 11 April Mahon returned to Eastbourne and moved Emily's large travelling trunk to the bungalow. He then returned to London, apparently to make arrangements to secure a passport but on Saturday, 12 April, he went to an ironmonger's shop in Victoria and bought a large cook's knife and a carpenter's saw.

He returned to Eastbourne and Emily, and the two were together in the bungalow for the next three nights. On Tuesday evening, 15 April, Emily Kaye met her fate.

Afterwards Mahon swore that her death was an accident, the result of a quarrel about their future and that she had fallen heavily and hit her head.

Mahon dragged the body into the spare bedroom and locked the door. The next day he returned to London, met Ethel Duncan and

This special sketch of the scene of the bungalow crime, with an X marking the spot, was published by the Eastbourne Gazette on 7th May 1924.

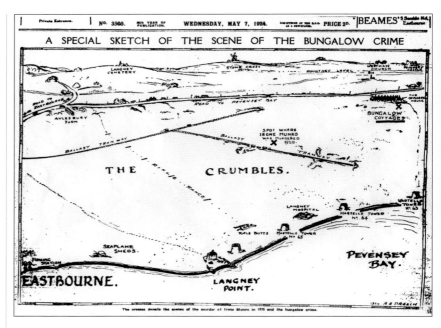

took her out to dinner. Incredibly he invited her to spend the coming Easter weekend with him at the bungalow on the Crumbles, to which the unsuspecting girl agreed.

On the morning of Good Friday Mahon was back in Eastbourne and a further horror began. He dismembered Emily's body with the saw and knife bought in London and the dreadful parcels were put in Emily's trunk in the spare bedroom.

In the evening Mahon met Ethel Duncan at Eastbourne station and they spent the weekend together at the bungalow. Ethel saw the trunk in the spare bedroom and Mahon said it was full of valuable books he was looking after for a friend. While she was there he screwed up the door. Ethel Duncan did not find his behaviour suspicious and on Easter Monday she returned to her home in London.

During the following week Mahon built a fire in the sitting room grate and burned Emily Kaye's head, which had been severed from the body. Other parts followed, disposed of in the same way, then the torso was further dismembered and boiled in stewpans in the kitchen so that they could be cut into smaller pieces. Mahon put most of these last remains into a Gladstone bag and threw them from the carriage window of a train when he later travelled to Waterloo Station in London.

It was then that he made the first and only mistake in his cold and methodical plans. He left the Gladstone bag at the left luggage office at Waterloo station and while he was away from home on the weekend of 25 April his wife searched the pockets of his suit and found the cloakroom ticket.

Mavourneen had been worried by his absence over the two previous weekends and believed he might be frequenting racecourses and returning to his old ways. She said nothing to her husband but enlisted the help of a private investigator, John Beard.

On 1 May they went together to Waterloo and retrieved the Gladstone bag. Beard was no fool and although the bag was locked he probed into one end and found something that prompted him to call Scotland Yard. When the police arrived they took a small piece of cloth from the bag which revealed human blood. Mavourneen was sent home, still unaware of the find, to return the cloakroom ticket to Mahon's suit.

Now a trap was set. Two detectives kept watch on the left luggage office and on 2 May Mahon collected the bag prior to another trip to Eastbourne. As soon as it was in his possession the police pounced and Mahon was taken to Cannon Row police station and confronted by the contents, which included a few pieces of blood stained clothing, a large cook's knife and a canvas tennis racket bag with the initials E.B.K.

He remained cool and told the police he supposed 'he had carried meat home for the dogs' in the bag, but finally after hours of interrogation he admitted the death of Emily Kaye and his disposal of the body.

Two police inspectors were sent to Eastbourne to the Officer's House and what they found there was a scene described by the experienced Home Office pathologist, Bernard Spilsbury, as the most gruesome he had ever come across. There was a terrible stench in the small bungalow as four parcels still remained in the trunk in the bedroom.

The presence of the police and the pathologist soon became known and while Spilsbury made his painstaking study of what was left of poor Emily Kaye, a task which took eight hours, a crowd of horrified people gathered outside.

On the following Tuesday Mahon was charged with murder at Hailsham magistrates court and the next day an inquest was held at the bungalow, attended by Mahon at his request.

A thousand sightseers surrounded the building, booing and jeering as the accused man was led in under heavy police escort.

Strenuous efforts to find other parts of the body were made but despite searching nearby areas and digging up the garden of the cottage, nothing was found.

The inquest resumed in May and Patrick Mahon was sent for trial at Lewes Assizes on 15 July.

Sir Henry Curtis Bennett led for the prosecution and Mr. J.D. Cassels defended Patrick Mahon. The unfortunate Ethel Duncan, considerably distressed, spent an hour in the witness box and maintained she had seen nothing to arouse her suspicion during the weekend she spent with Mahon. As the trial continued and the macabre story unfolded two jury men collapsed. They were replaced and Mahon gave evidence for more than five hours.

The story he told was of a woman infatuated with him and one who had drawn him reluctantly into an affair. He told the court on the evening of Emily's death they had a furious quarrel and according to him he was attacked by his lover.

At this point he broke down in tears and still sobbing went on to relate that in the struggle they fell and Emily's head hit the coal scuttle. This, he said, must have caused her death and, because he was in a state of fear and shock he remembered little of the next hours except that he went outside. When he returned he panicked and decided to conceal everything.

At the end of this dramatic story Mahon's counsel asked him, 'Did you desire the death of Miss Kaye?'

Mahon, calm again, replied: 'Never at any time'.

The defence did its best to plead that Mahon was the victim of extraordinary circumstances rather than cold hearted murderer, but members of the jury, who had no knowledge of his previous record, were not convinced.

The cause of death given by the accused man was refuted by the pathologist who said a fall on a coal scuttle would not have caused injuries that would have had such a rapidly fatal result.

Most damning of all for the jury's opinion of Mahon's character was his assignation with Ethel Duncan, at a time when he had a wife and child at home and a mistress in a bungalow at Eastbourne. He was found guilty of murder.

The bungalow on the Crumbles became a strange tourist attraction when the lease was taken over by a group of entrepreneurs of doubtful taste but sound business instinct. Visitors were charged a shilling each for guided tours of the cottage and as the queues increased cold drinks were served from the front gate. There was considerable local protest and for two weeks the bungalow was closed, only to open again with the entrance fee in-creased to 1s 2d as coachloads of the curious continued to arrive.

Mahon's wife Mavourneen, remained loyal to the end and before his execution on Wednesday, 3 September, he wrote a kind and loving letter to her from his cell. The 'Officers House' on the Crumbles was demolished in 1953.

Patrick Mahon.

8. CALM AND STORM

The 1930s was a decade of contrasts. Despite economic depression there was a feeling of peace and stability overlying the hard times. A great many houses were built and on the beachland of the Crumbles, Hall and Company, later known as Hall Aggregates, took over the lease for gravel extraction in 1931.

As had happened in the past part of the Crumbles great store of shingle was put to use as building materials for new roads and houses. The output of the workings was some 250,000 tons a year and at first only the surface was removed. For more than a hundred years in all shingle was taken for railway ballast and later for building materials. As a result a large area of the great beach was reduced by twelve feet of its original height within 100 yards of the high water mark at the shore.

After the Ballast Line was closed a belt grading system was installed, the working plant a familiar sight to everyone who lived locally or passed by on the Pevensey Bay Road. The rhythmic clanking and tumbling of the pebbles up the steep incline of the belt track continued daily, the graded gravel then being taken away by road transport.

In the 1950s deeper gravel pits were dug, eventually becoming fresh water lakes, as the Crumbles still receives the drainage waters from the countryside. Hall Aggregates eventually closed the works when plans for the harbour development were agreed and the main plant was finally removed in 1986.

Between the wars the old Crumbles pond had been transformed into a boating lake at a cost of £10,000, a large sum in those days. It was described as 'madness' and a 'reckless waste of money' but the idea caught on and by the 1930s the pond had been drained and relined and become a popular lake in the Gilbert Recreation Grounds, now Princes Park. During the excavations the pond's great age was confirmed by the removal of two feet of sedge peat. Sluice gates at each end allowed the waters from interconnecting streams of the levels to drain into the lake and then under the shore road and beach into the sea.

On the eastern reaches of the Crumbles there was new building

One of the Oyster bungalows built in the Thirties at Beachlands. For a time it was comedian, Spike Milligan's, holiday home.

in Pevensey Bay – once known as the hamlet of Wallsend. It was here that the reclaimed land of the marshes met the shingle of the Crumbles and from a few cottages and farm buildings a small but thriving seaside village has evolved with a resident population today of more than 3,000.

In 1934 building continued eastwards in an area aptly known as Beachlands. Bungalows were advertised at 'from £495' and Beachlands now extends almost to Normans Bay.

On the lower level, behind the beach, there are bungalows and houses, among them the fascinating Oyster bungalows, so typical of the architecture of the period. They have flat roofs and circular designed frontages with big windows to admit the maximum amount of light and air. Stars of stage and screen in pursuit of privacy, among them Peter Sellars, Spike Milligan and members of the Crazy Gang, had homes in Pevensey Bay. A less reputable resident was train robber Ronald Biggs.

As Pevensey Bay grew there were continuing worries about erosion. It was estimated in 1936 that 160 feet of beach had been swept away in the previous four years and at high tides there had been some flooding.

By the end of the Thirties the rumble of Hitler's Germany could no longer be ignored. Britain's prime minister, Neville Chamberlain,

Eastbourne lifeboatmen and firemen fighting the blaze on the Barnhill. Photo: Eastbourne Library.

tried appeasement and negotiation, but to no avail. As Hitler's armies poured into Poland Britain declared war on Germany. Britain's coastline was under threat again and Eastbourne, together with other seaside towns, was in the front line.

The first bombing raids on coastal towns and on shipping in the Channel began in 1940. The Crumbles was the scene in the closing stages of a drama that began in the late evening of 20 March, of that year. A 5,439 ton British merchant ship, the *Barnhill*, laden with copper and general cargo from Halifax, Nova Scotia, was bombed by a lone Dornier three miles south west of Beachy Head.

The Eastbourne lifeboat, the *Jane Holland*, soon reached the stricken ship, which was on fire, and took twenty eight men back to shore. Four crewmen had been killed in the attack and a fifth man died later in hospital. Seven other men were injured but survived.

There was no sign of the captain, Michael O'Neill, and the survivors believed he had been killed on the wrecked bridge. In fact he had been blown off the bridge, landing unconscious on the foredeck. When he came to O'Neill found he was the only man on board and in spite of his considerable injuries he managed to crawl along the deck to the fo'c'sle where by clenching the rope in his teeth, he rang the ship's bell. The clanging was heard by the

crew of the tug *Foremost* from Newhaven and the lifeboat was recalled from Eastbourne.

Back came the *Jane Holland* in early dawn to find a heavy sea running. Two crew members, Alec Huggett and Thomas Allchorn, boarded the *Barnhill* from the tug. This was an act of great courage and daring for, as described by another rescuer: 'at one moment the ship would be towering above us showering sparks and molten lead and the next we would be riding on the wave almost level with the *Barnhill*'.

Once aboard the lifeboatmen made their way forward, playing water with the fire hose of the tug on the decks to keep off the flames. The lifeboat was brought alongside so that the doctor on board could shout instructions to Huggett and Allchorn.

Carefully the injured captain was lowered to the lifeboat and returned to shore, where he was taken to hospital. The *Jane Holland* took to sea again with members of the Eastbourne Fire Brigade and they and the crew of the tug continued to fight the fire. But now the wind and sea had control and slowly the *Barnhill* drifted past the beaches of Eastbourne, watched by hundreds of people on the seafront, eventually running aground south east of Langney Point on the shore of the Crumbles.

In the following weeks cargo from the ruptured holds drifted

51

ashore, hastened by heavy seas which continued to break up the ship. People who walked to the Crumbles shore to see the beached wreck found tins of food floating at the water's edge.

The labels had washed off so no one knew if the tins contained meat or soup, fruit or beans, but everyone salvaged as many as possible for their cupboards at home. This was against the law and an official notice in the Eastbourne Gazette in April sternly warned: 'Nothing must be taken from the Beach'.

Suddenly a number of abandoned cheeses appeared all over the Crumbles, and after that the tins were considered fair game. Of the remainder of the Barnhill's cargo a considerable tonnage was saved by official salvage but while the salvage crews worked a further bombing attack was made on the beached hulk. Fortunately the bombs fell into the sea and the German bomber was seen off by a British fighter plane. A part of the ship's superscructure was removed before the gallant *Barnhill* finally broke up, her stern swinging round and sinking into deeper water.

Captain O'Neill recovered and visited Eastbourne in June, 1941 to pay tribute to his rescuers. He said that he owed his life to Alec Huggett, Tom Allchorn and the crew of the *Jane Holland*.

'But for the brave men of this town', he said, 'my men and myself would never have got ashore. They risked everything to get aboard my blazing ship'. Alec Huggett and Thomas Allchorn were awarded the Royal National Lifeboat Institution's bronze medal and a framed Letter of Appreciation went to Coxswain Hardy.

Today the rusted boilers of the *Barnhill* can be seen at low tide from the shore of the Crumbles, rounded shapes of metal that are now a favoured resting place for cormorants. Beneath the shallow water lie steel plates of the wrecked ship and for many years on the shingle ridge near to the Martello tower stood the buoy, pictured right, that was used in the salvage operations. Memorials to the courage of the merchant seamen during the war and to the RNLI.

With the bombing of the *Barnhill* Eastbourne had received a sober foretaste of things to come. France fell and in the early summer of 1940 the British and French forces fell back to the beaches of Dunkirk. The Eastbourne lifeboat and other local fishing and pleasure boats took part in the bold rescue operation to recover the stranded men and the *Jane Holland* was machine-gunned and abandoned. She was later found drifting near

Dover and was then repaired and returned to service in Eastbourne a year later.

After Dunkirk the air attack on Britain increased in ferocity. Hitler's plans for invasion of England were delayed to gain supremacy in the air. The Battle of Britain began in the summer of 1940 and reached its climax in the autumn. Despite heavy losses the German invasion plans, code named Operation Sea Lion, were thwarted and eventually abandoned. These plans had included a landing at Cuckmere Haven and almost inevitably, at Pevensey Bay on the low, inviting shores of the Crumbles.

Concrete tank traps were constructed across the shingle in the area near Langney Point. All along the coast beaches were closed, mines were laid and miles of barbed wire defences festooned the shoreline. The old Seaplane Sheds on the Crumbles became an ARP post and pill boxes were built near the shore. The Martello towers were fortified with gunnery stations and the Wish Tower on

The buoy that was used in the Barhills' salvage operations.

its rise of ground became an important anti-aircraft gunnery post. At Pevensey Castle a machine gun post was built on the south east ramparts of the old Roman wall and at Beachy Head a radar station was established.

The first bombing raids on Eastbourne were possibly initial attacks on a town which would have been a vital defence and communications centre in the area of planned landing of German troops. Over the Channel came the Dorniers, Jumkers and Heinkels and dropped high explosives and incendiaries on the town.

The blitz on London began in the later months of 1940. To bomb cities with ports and factories was an obvious part of the enemy strategy but for some reason Eastbourne continued to be the target of bombing raids throughout the war. Perhaps there was a lingering thought of an invasion in the area but whatever the reason the small town was hard hit and there was little respite.

First it was the fighter bombers in the daytime, followed by a period of night bombing raids and in 1944 came the flying bombs. The V1s, nicknamed doodlebugs, were launched from France and intended to reach London but did not always do so. Eastbourne was on the flight path of these rocket propelled missiles, and the more sophisticated V2s which followed them. The sound of the whirring noisy approach which suddenly cut off for a moment of silence before the inevitable explosion became an everyday background of dread.

Victory in Europe in 1945 was followed by the surrender of Japan in 1946 and the world wide conflict was over. In Eastbourne the cost had been high. It was officially declared to be the town that had suffered more bombing attacks than any other in the south east region. There had been 112 air raids, with thousands of houses damaged, and 475 totally destroyed. No part of the town escaped and bombs even fell on the empty stretches of the Crumbles, one near the present day Sovereign Centre.

Civilian casualties numbered more than 1,000 of which 174 were fatal. This figure would have been higher but for the evacuation of children and adults that could be spared which reduced the population of the town to an estimated 13,000, compared to about 60,000 in 1939.

With the ending of the war the beaches were cleared of mines and barbed wire. Most of the concrete tank traps on the Crumbles were demolished and removed. The miles of golden pebbles that had presented a favoured landing place for enemy forces were safe once again.

....

Tram No. 3 at the eastern terminus of Eastbourne Tramway in 1954. It is one of the original small vehicles from Rhyl, which were adapted to the two foot gauge. Photo: S.C. Nash.

9. NEW DEVELOPMENTS

When the war was over rebuilding and renovation began and as the economy recovered new housing projects were built for the ever increasing population. By the 1960s urban development again encroached on the Crumbles but before that the shingle land was virtually left untouched. People went to the foreland to picnic, to gather flowers and blackberries, to skate on the shallow frozen ponds in the winter and in the summer there was often a fair.

In 1954 the Eastbourne Tramway Company opened and delightful little trams ran along the sea frontage from the Royal Parade to the Crumbles via Princes Park. They were the brainchild of Mr. C.W. Lane, an engineer and business man who had built two remarkable scale models which were originally run at the Voryd Amusement Park in Rhyl with great success.

A third model was built and the popularity of the tramway in Rhyl prompted thoughts of operating one on the south coast. Eastbourne Corporation was approached and after a demonstration and tests permission was granted to construct a tramway to a depot near Wartling Road. Work on laying the two foot gauge track began in March, 1954 and was completed by July.

Two of Mr. Lane's original trams were rebuilt to the new gauge for service in Eastbourne and two new trams were built, No. 238 being specially designed and a replica of Blackpool Corporation's modern eight wheel double decker closed top trams with a centre entrance.

The official opening of the line's first full season came at Whitsun, 1955. The ceremony was performed by the mayor and covered by BBC television on film, one of the trams being converted into a studio for the occasion. Thus suitably launched the Eastbourne Tramway immediately proved to be a popular attraction and later the route was extended to a point on the Crumbles midway to Langney Point.

In the summer season queues were always waiting at both ends of the line for rides. Tram No. 3 was very popular with its open top deck so a further tram was designed exclusively for the Eastbourne tramway. This was No. 6, an open top double deck type with standard size seats provided for forty passengers. The second Eastbourne tram was No. 7, similar to No. 6 but with two short saloons at either end of the lower deck. No. 4 was of a modern single deck design with a central entrance. In addition to the normal hand and electric brakes it was also fitted with air operated brakes and air whistles.

A reserve tram was built for the Eastbourne fleet, another open top double decker with end saloons boasting spacious access to the upper deck incorporating a landing midway. This one broke away from the standard livery of green and cream and was painted in shades of red and white and parts for the new model were taken from old trams which had operated as far apart as London and Glasgow. With its spanking new fleet in operation the company had no further use for the miniature trams that had begun the venture and they were withdrawn from service. Three were sold and shipped to the USA and No. 226 was kept as a works car and numbered 01 in the Eastbourne fleet.

The route started near Princes Park gates. A single track line ran east alongside the road then turned north into Princes Park where a sharp turn brought it to the Golf House and the first passing loop. Beyond that the track singled again and bore right and left out of the park and on to the Crumbles where it became a double track before crossing the road and passing the depot. Another loop continued to the works but the single track beyond the depot went on towards Wartling Road, now Prince William Parade, running parallel until the terminus was reached midway to Langney Point. Here people could alight to walk to the point for the stunning views of the coast from Beachy Head to the Hastings cliffs.

The track itself consisted of flat bottomed rail spiked to transverse wooden sleepers, except at road crossings where grooved tramway rail with metal tie bars was used and laid on concrete edged with granite setts. The trams were driven by electric power from overhead lines, the electricity supplied from a generating plant under the offices of the works building which also supplied voltage for the lighting along the tramway and for traction purposes.

Most people boarded the trams at the Royal Parade terminus and a 10d return ticket took them to the terminus on the Crumbles. Along the way there were Stop and Request places and

some of the signs were antiques given by various people.

The service operated daily between 10am to 10pm from Whitsun until September and then at weekends only until Christmas and between Easter and Whitsun.

For many years the Crumbles tramway was a much loved feature of the town, used by thousands of visitors and residents. But times move on and the face of the Crumbles changed as new housing development progressed. Operation of the Eastbourne Tramway eventually ceased in 1969 and the trams were moved to Seaton in Devon where they continue to be used for pleasure rides.

Building of the Langney Point estate began in the 1960s when new methods of concrete piles and rafts were utilised to provide a firm foundation on the considerable depth of shingle.

A wide main road bisected the estate where Princes Road led to the sea and to the new swimming pool which was later extended to become the Sovereign Centre, a venue for fitness and leisure activities. Young families and retired people were attracted to the new estate with its parade of shops and pleasant village atmosphere close to the sea.

When the tramway was extended larger cars were built. This is No 7 making one of the last runs in Last Trams Week, 1969. Photo: S.C. Nash

East of Princes Park the level of the land had been lowered considerably by the old shingle extractions and this was now infilled to become a grassy recreation area – the Five Acres playing fields. In the north east corner near the busy roundabout the lower level still exists where a small woodland of trees and shrubs borders the stream that flows from the levels to the Princes Park lake.

The spread of new building meant that the sewage outfall at Langney Point, which only extended 180 feet from the shore, had to be renewed. In 1965 a new £500,000 outfall scheme was approved and an underground pumping station built with a new pipeline reaching out 2,500ft from the shore. The waste disposal works could deal with forty million gallons a day and at the time this all seemed highly satisfactory. However, Eastbourne and Pevensey continued to grow. More buildings and more people. Higher standards of anti pollution rules meant that by the 1990s another new outfall was being considered.

Langney Point estate had extended east and south to the sea frontage and building had begun on the harbour and marina development on the Crumbles. Fierce discussions took place as to the site of a new waste disposal works. Should it be an inland treatment works or again discharge into the sea? Finally planning permission was given for the £42.5million scheme to be built at Langney Point, with an underground treatment works and an outfall pipe 3.2km out to sea.

Dredgers scooped out a trench on the sea bed and a barge with a great winch pulled a new pipeline into position which was then covered with a smooth domed layer of concrete. The beach headworks included a treatment process fourteen metres below ground level, a sophisticated procedure which promised no more pungent smells. The access building is constructed in the rounded shape of a Napoleonic fort to blend in with the surroundings and the old outfall remains in place to be used to discharge excess stormwater into the sea.

The final stage was to improve the access road at beach level for the local fishing boats and to landscape and establish a nature reserve on the environmentally valuable stretch of the old Crumbles land between Prince William Parade and the foreshore.

The sixty years that have passed since the end of the Second World War have seen continuing social and political change and amazing scientific and technological advances. Now the Crumbles has seen a final invasion of its land as an ambitious harbour and marina development moves towards completion.

10. THE HARBOUR AND MARINA

The idea of a harbour at Eastbourne was first suggested more than a hundred years ago when two possible sites were considered, the shore near Holywell or the Crumbles. At that time lack of funds for such a major project presented a stumbling block that could not be overcome but the idea was not forgotten and Eastbourne's harbour eventually became a reality.

By 1966 the cost of a harbour at the Crumbles was estimated at £500,000 but no one could be found to invest such a large sum of money. However the scheme was favoured by the Trustees of the Compton Estates, owner of the land, and a harbour village was incorporated in the 1967 Eastbourne urban plan.

In 1975 a Harbour Bill went before Parliament only to be blocked by Labour M.Ps. In spite of this setback in 1979 research costing £250,000 was undertaken on plans for a now multi million harbour and waterside housing scheme and in August 1980 the Harbour Bill came before the House of Commons once again and after a debate of three hours it was passed with a majority of 180 to twelve.

Having gained parliamentary permission the old bugbear of lack of financial backing reared its head. Plans were shelved because of rises in construction costs. An estimate of £9.5 million in 1975 had risen to £24 million by 1980.

In 1986 a joint statement from Tarmac Construction and the Chatsworth Trustees announced plans for a £200million scheme at the Crumbles of an outer harbour, an inner marina and a development of about 2,000 homes, with a hotel at the mouth of the proposed harbour complex. The scene was set, the plans made, but it was to be five more years before construction work got under way.

Gradually problems were ironed out. Hydraulic research was undertaken and assurances given that any depletion of the beaches would be replaced. Some problems could not be resolved. The size of the project meant that the remaining natural areas of the Crumbles would be lost and all that the developers could promise was an area of preserved land within the new estates.

*The shore east of
Langney Point
before the harbour
excavation work
started.*

In 1988 the Chatsworth Trustees pulled out of financial backing and the harbour site of 330 acres was sold to the giant Tarmac EZD and at the same time thirty acres were sold to the Asda group for the retail park to be built on the northern boundary of the site.

An amended Harbour Bill had its third and final reading and it was passed by the Lords after Tarmac had promised to put aside £2million to help foot the cost of future beach erosion should it occur. This was the final chapter in the long saga of negotiations and soon the building began.

A large area of land was levelled for the retail shopping park adjacent to Pevensey Bay Road and the new Asda superstore opened in 1989. The shopping complex included a six screen multiplex cinema and other retail stores. On the wider reaches of the Crumbles, engineers made calculations and set markers but before excavations could begin the water table had to be lowered by pumping out water from the Crumbles down to nine metres below sea level.

The National River Authority rescued fish from the lakes and removed them to nearby rivers and ponds and in October 1991 work on the harbour began in earnest. The people of Eastbourne flocked to Langney Point in their hundreds to watch the main contractors, Kier Construction, start on the two harbour arms and the excavations for the harbour itself.

For the harbour arms, which had to protect the outer harbour from the prevailing winds, 160,000 tonnes of rock were brought from Norway by massive barges and these arrived at Langney Point every ten days.

They became a familiar sight, together with the small sturdy tugboats that amazingly controlled the enormous weight of the barges and their cargo. Great rumblings were heard as the loads were dropped in place and lorries were used to move the huge rocks to their proper positions. This work went on daily for more than a year until the harbour arms were completed.

From the walkways on the shoreline could also be seen the deep excavations of the inner and outer harbours. In 1992 a Polegate firm specialising in concrete work contracted to build the twin

Tugs bringing in one of the giant barges loaded with rock from Norway.

locks together with the lining of the harbour and the channels which would lead to waterside housing. One hundred men worked on the concreting from dawn to dusk and the task was completed in record time.

In November 1992 the gates for the twin locks were lowered into place. Made in Newcastle by Pearson Reelotech the eight curved gates were the largest purpose built marina lock gates in the United Kingdom. Each outer gate is 11.5m high and weighs 25 tonnes, controlled by means of hydraulic cylinders. Linking the outer tidal harbour to the inner marina, 3m below sea level, the 150ft long and 50ft wide locks could allow 100 boats to move through every hour. The main work was now complete and in February 1993 the entrance was dug out and the sea flooded quietly into the new harbour.

On 6 May 1993 the first boats went through the lock gates. The Eastbourne lifeboat of that time, the *Duke of Kent*, was the first boat to go in and out of the lock gates officially and was now to be permanently moored at the outer harbour, giving easier access to

Work in progress on the lock gates in 1993.

The inner harbour showing the Earl of Zetland, Eastbourne's first floating bar and restaurant.

the sea than the old launching site at Royal Parade.

The new harbour was named the Sovereign Harbour because of the long association of Eastbourne with the Royal Sovereign light in the Channel. By July of 1993 more than half the berths were let and the harbour had seen 2,000 visiting boats, among the first to sail in a flotilla of yachts from Le Treport on the French coast near Dieppe.

Now in the marina there is always a forest of masts, the wind singing in the rigging of the beautiful sailing yachts. The pace of life is slow and easy as the boats come and go and people stand at the lock gates and walk round the inner and outer harbours for there is always something of interest to watch. Fishing boats use the harbour facilities as well as the pleasure craft and the harbour is open twenty four hours a day, 365 days of the year, with visitors berths always available.

Between 1996 and 2006 development continued of what is destined to become one of the largest composite marinas in

Europe. The cost of the infrastructure of harbour and roads alone is estimated at £60million. As the harbour village nears completion there will be berths for up to 1,300 vessels and some 3,000 homes, which include detached houses, apartment blocks, town houses and waterside dwellings with mooring facilities.

The first boat to use the dock of the inner harbour was the *Earl of Zetland*, moored for use as a floating bar and restaurant. For thirty years the ship was used as a passenger ferry between Aberdeen and the Shetlands and Orkneys. During the war she plied the Pentland Firth as a troopship, steaming more than 160,000 miles and carrying 600,000 soldiers. In 1975, renamed the *Celtic Surveyor* and used as a diving support ship, she then became a survey ship in the North Sea oilfields, before being converted into an entertainment vessel in Great Yarmouth in 1983.

More than £1million was spent on converting the ship and she became a favourite place for visitors to the inner harbour for several years until she had to leave before development began in 1999 of the Waterfront, an equally popular venue with its shops and restaurants. The Earl of Zetland now has a permanent home

Eastbourne lifeboat passing through the outer harbour.

at the Royal Quay, North Shields, on the river Tyne.

Two Martello towers stand near the sea on the harbour site. No. 64, once a lonely sentinel between Langney Point and Pevensey is now surrounded by dwellings and will be preserved, as will the tower at Langney Point, which was used for many years as a Coastguard lookout post. Close to this historic tower is still open ground, the preferred area for a hotel or tourist facilities in the future.

One of the most important vessels in the new harbour is undoubtedly the Eastbourne lifeboat. In 1993 a new boat, the *Royal Thames*, arrived to replace the older *Duke of Kent* She was partly funded by the Royal Thames Yacht Club and the rest of the money came from a £200,000 fund raising appeal backed by the *Eastbourne Herald*.

Everyone who lived near the sea in Eastbourne was familiar with the sound of the distress signal as the rockets were sent up, exploding at a height of 600 to 700 feet in the air, with first a puff of smoke and a flash of light, then the sound reverberating a few seconds later. This old tradition has been discontinued for safety reasons and will only be used in future if the electronic pagers or mobile phones of the crew should fail.

Coastguard helicopters from Lee on Solent join the lifeboat crew two or three times a year for difficult rescues and training exercises are regularly held with these helicopters and RAF Sea Kings from Suffolk.

The smaller inshore lifeboat with its crew of two or three is still stationed at Royal Parade, near Princes Park. The Royal Thames goes out from the harbour with a crew of seven and these dedicated men answer between 80 and 90 call outs each year. This figure has reduced from an average of 120 call outs in past years as boat and yacht owners become more aware of safety issues from information and talks given by the RNLI.

In 1994 a £100,000 legacy provided a new lifeboat station near the lock gates. The compact two storey boathouse includes a crew training room and an operations room. Now the men return to a warm place where gear and boots can dry quickly and a haven too when necessary for shipwrecked mariners, yachtsmen in trouble, bathers caught by dangerous currents and everyone else they save from the perils of the sea.

PART II. THE NATURAL HISTORY
1. ORIGINS AND FORMATION

Shingle forelands, unlike most headlands which are composed or hard rock that offers a strong resistance to the sea, are developed by longshore or onshore drift. This is a mysterious progression of shingle to the shore from deposits on the seabed or along the coast.

Langney Point and the Crumbles are classic examples of this type of formation and came into being in the same way as other areas of shingle deposits. The foreland of Dungeness, the Chesil Beach in Dorset, the Looe Bar in Cornwall and the high shingle banks of the north Norfolk coast are all monuments to the power of the sea. In Sussex the Shoreham beach is a further example and behind this beach is a lagoon, which is often a feature of shingle barriers.

The Crumbles has its own history of construction. Changes in sea level have occurred mainly as a result of the growth and wane of the ice ages. The level of the sea has been both higher and lower than it is now and has left raised or submerged features as a result.

During the last glacial period the sea left the Channel and the shoreline stretched between Brittany and Cornwall, the Channel area becoming a valley, the site of a vast drainage system of rivers known as the Solent/Seine system, flowing west to the Atlantic coast.

The rivers carried eroded material of rock and gravel from their sources and along their routes. When the period of glaciation ended and the ice began to melt the sea level rose once again, probably by more than 100 metres in the last 14,000 years. The sea returned to flood the Channel and establish the straits of Dover.

During the last 10,000 years the sea level has risen by 45m. Deposits of gravel on the sea floor left by the river systems of the last ice age have become part of the construction material of the shingle lands that have appeared and disappeared on the coast in this long period of time.

Recent research using borehole sinkings and radio carbon analysis have revealed an interesting history of the area of the

Crumbles. Ten thousand years ago a great barrier of sandbanks and dunes began to form close to Langney Point. In the following 1,000 years the tidal inlets behind these dunes were blocked and the area of the Willingdon levels became a woodland of pine and hazel trees, with salt marshes behind the sands. On the dunes juniper bushes grew and as the climate warmed the Willingdon woodland extended its range of trees to include oaks and elms.

Then the sand banks were swept away and the sea invaded the low lying land to its greatest extent. This was a time of bay and estuary that lasted for 4,000 years with a shallow offshore zone of sand banks covered by the sea.

About 3,400 years ago a second formation of extensive spits and banks of sand and possibly some shingle, came into existence close to St. Anthony's hill and the slopes surrounding the levels were covered by a forest of trees. Then the sea invaded once again and for centuries the Willingdon and Pevensey levels became estuarine.

The Crumbles is the third barrier that has formed across this area of low lying land which for the last 10,000 years has been mainly covered by the sea. The gradual erosion of the chalk cliffs nearby, which have receded by an estimated 4km during the Holocene and the effects of longshore drift from the south west were probably the contributing factors in the foundation of the Crumbles.

At some time during the last 2,000 years shingle spits evolved across the entrance to the old embayment which in Roman times had a bed of alluvial silt brought down by the rivers that flowed to the sea. When the waters of the rivers met the tide the speed of the water lessened, allowing mud and silt to settle in a bar across the entrance to the bay. Here the drifting shingle began to settle, eventually establishing a continuous line of new beachland with outlets to the sea just west of St. Anthony's Hill. As the shingle bank grew these outlets later moved eastwards to Pevensey.

From about the eleventh century the Crumbles developed rapidly into a vast beach and by the early 1600s it measured two miles from its northern boundary – now marked by the Pevensey Bay Road – to the shoreline.

It is thought unlikely that longshore drift alone could account for this further accumulation of shingle and that the main source came from offshore beds, part of the gravels from the rivers of the Channel valley of the last ice age.

The great beach stretched from Eastbourne to Normans Bay, its formation enabling the Willingdon and Pevensey levels to be reclaimed from the sea. But then the wind and waves began to steal it away and slowly the coastline receded.

The marked erosion of the Crumbles between 1610 and 1785 suggests that the supply of offshore shingle had come to an end. The south westerly winds curved the shore to a point which moved eastwards to the site of Langney Point as it is today.

The continuing recession of the shoreline was illustrated by the fate of the Martello towers. In 1818 three towers west of Langney Point stood 177ft inshore from the high water mark but by 1852 the sea had taken them. Longshore drift steadily plundered the Crumbles beach, moving it along the coast to Hastings and Dungeness. In 1926 the sea broke through the beach west of Langney Point and poured into the Crumbles pond. It was only by stopping the breach before the next high tide that a serious flooding was averted.

The long years of erosion were finally halted by the building of timber groynes but the sea level continues to rise, although very slowly, and the supply of shingle from longshore drift is not sufficient to maintain this important sea defence. When the storms of winter deplete the beaches they are now replenished with shingle brought in by barge and in 1994 a £17million scheme was begun to replace the old groynes that have served the Crumbles

Coastline changes at Eastbourne since 1610. Diagram courtesy of S. Jennings.

shore so well. For although shingle can be moved by the sea it is an excellent defence. Whereas sea walls must withstand the crash of waves against them they also have the effect of creating a powerful backwash which pulls away the beach. A shingle bank provides the means for incoming breaking waves to be dispersed by sinking down through the pebbles.

The present depth of the thousand of tons of shingle that constitute the Crumbles foreland varies but at Langney Point the measurement is six metres deep and below that is another ten metres of sand. At the shore the rise of beach is a further two metres above Ordinance Datum – the mean level of the sea between high and low tides.

Millions of pebbles make up the Crumbles land. These smooth stones, honed to perfection by long years in the sea, have a pleasing variety of shape and colour. There are shades of blue and grey, white, black, pink, brown and orange. Stones of chalk and flint which come from the cliffs of the South Downs. Also chert, sandstone, some igneous rock and even quartz and quartz tourmalines that may have travelled from the pebble beds at Budleigh Salterton far to the west.

The movement of shingle shores is a continuing process controlled by the sea and prevailing currents. It is estimated that it takes 120 years for eroded material to travel by longshore drift from Cornwall to Sussex. The growth of the Crumbles from the first drift of pebbles settling on a bar of mud to the vast beach of the 1600s and finally to the curved shore and beachland that exists today is a fine example of the sea's creation.

In the normal course of events this barrier may have eventually been swept away, as were its predecessors, but human ingenuity has found the means of thwarting further erosion. The remaining land of the Crumbles is safe from the hungry sea.

2. THE SHINGLE HABITAT

For many years the Crumbles was quite simply a naturalist's paradise, considered one of the premier sites in Sussex. The position of a foreland – untouched by pesticides – in a wide bay sheltered by Beachy Head provided ideal conditions for a myriad species of plants, insects, birds and small animals.

The original shallow ridges were colonised by communities of lichen and mosses. The lichens found on the northern boundary of the Crumbles are thought to be the latest generation of a community established some 800 years ago. Other plants typical to shingle habitat have been abundant, encouraged by the fine silt of inland drainage mixed with the pebbles and humus material from the dead vegetation of each succeeding year.

The plants are home and food source for insects, including some rare varieties. The insects in turn attract the birds, who feed on them and on the seed heads of the plants. Stony ground is ideal for

In winter the old ridges on the Crumbles could be clearly seen.

a basking grass snake or lizard and as the vegetation increased small mammals found a home. So the chain grew as the predators appeared – sparrowhawk, crow, magpie and the ubiquitous fox.

For the first fifty years of the 20th century the open land of the Crumbles stretched from Princes Park to Pevensey. Removal of shingle lowered the surface of the inland areas by about twelve feet.

To the purist the undisturbed shingle was of the greater interest but nature has a way of adapting to interference. The lower surfaces offered more shelter and were closer to the level of the water table. Reed beds and marshy pools appeared and thorn scrub, willow, elder and bramble found a foothold giving cover and nesting places for a great variety of birds.

The open spaces have disappeared now but for thirty years the area east of Langney Point remained as a beautiful natural garden with the original 'fulls' near the shore and the lower surfaces attracting plants and flowers from the nearby downland.

Seven large gravel pits dug out in previous years filled with fresh water and soon aquatic plants encouraged stickleback, roach and perch. These lakes of deep calm water became a safe haven and hunting ground for water birds and the steep banks a site for plants, the older lakes fringed by rushes and wild iris.

It is difficult to evaluate the population of wild life that existed on the Crumbles but records were kept, notably by Miss M.A. Ash, a local teacher, for the Sussex Botanical Recording Society, and more than 400 botanical species were noted.

Experts in all fields of natural interested visited the Crumbles and a species list of 216 insects put the site high in value for the entymologist. The Sussex Bird Reports give a long list of species recorded, but never complete because of the number of migrants.

During the winter months the vegetation died down and virtually disappeared, the long stretches of shingle bare and almost desolate under cold easterly winds.

With the onset of spring and the long days of summer an incredible transformation took place. Much of the shingle disappeared under a sea of waving grasses and a mass of flowering plants. On still days the air shimmered with warmth and colour, the only sounds the bird song and the low hum of insect life. In the season of plenty the shingle habitat revealed its treasures.

3. THE CRUMBLES FLORA

Before urban development extended east across the Crumbles the vegetation was mainly maritime flora specifically suited to shingle land. These plants are well adapted for life on stony ground, the larger varieties having long tap roots which give a firm hold and the means of finding nutrients and water deep below the surface. Small plants hug the ground and some of the general species of wild flowers can be found on shingle in prostrate form, flat on the ground. The foliage of maritime plants is often characterised by a distinctive grey green colour with fleshy leaves and stems which can retain water.

Areas of stable and established shingle near the shore showed a profusion of these specialised plants. The shallow ridges were divided into areas of small and large stones, creating different habitats. Depressions between the ridges provided a site for interesting heath communities of mosses and lichens, known as Lower Plants.

Twenty eight of these strange and beautiful species grew on the Crumbles and varieties of *Cladonia* and *Parmelia* were well represented together with rare and very scarce lichens.

Most of the varieties have leaves of a blueish grey or pale green, ranging from fluted and branched growths, reminiscent of seaweed, to the delicate mass of slender many branched stems of *Cladonia Portentosa*. Small flat scaly lichens could be seen on individual pebbles, the brilliant orange of the common *Xanthoria parietina* contrasting with the black spots which, although small, have the resounding name of *Parmelia glabrutula ssp, fuliginosa*. These tiny lichens stand out well on a white pebble and have a simple beauty of colour shape and form.

In early spring the sheltered area ridges showed the Mouse-ear Hawkweed, a small plant with flat leaves demonstrating its name, tiny stems supporting a single flower head of lemony yellow. Then came the glories of the Sea Campion. Low growing with a tight cushion of grey green leaves, each plant presents a mass of white flowers with a distinctive black dot from the calyx. The petals rise from a pink sepal and in May and early June the Crumbles literally

*Ragwort and
Wild Carrot on
the lakeside
shingle.*

shimmered with thousands of delicate plants in full bloom.

Summer brings the Yellow Horned Poppy, truly elegant, a plant on its own for there is nothing quite like it. Papery yellow poppy heads blend perfectly with the greyish green foliage and the seed heads are long and curved. During winter the flat ground hugging rosette of downy leaves is perfectly adapted to the environment but in summer the plant can grow to three feet.

Other coastal plants included Sea Kale, the Sea Radish and Sea Beet, the latter having long strong leaves of a brilliant green and well adapted to life by the sea. On the older parts of the Crumbles also grew a number of plants unusual on undisturbed shingle. Wild Carrot with its flat head of tightly packed white florets with one pink spot in the centre, Red Fescue, Ribworth Plantain and Buckshorn Plantain shared the pebbles with the more characteristic growth of Sheep's Sorrel, early Hair Grass and False Oat Grass.

Inland, on the lower excavated surfaces of the Crumbles shingle, many maritime flora were present and the shingle had settled to become host to an amazing variety of plants. First to appear were the Coltsfoot – great masses of brilliant yellow daisy like heads nodding on their neatly folded stems, mainly on the banks of the lakes. On flat areas of small pebbles brilliant yellow patches of Sedum Acre shared the ground with Haresfoot Clover, Kidney Vetch, Birdsfoot Trefoil and Scarlet Pimpernel, also the prostrate variety of Herb Robert.

Spring rains and longer days brought the white Melilot and the yellow Ribbed Melilot into growth and flower. The middle area of the horseshoe lake became a sea of Ox-Eye Daisies and everywhere Vipers Bugloss shot to its full height, the spiked stems of deep blue flowers sporting vermilion tinged stamens.

By mid summer all the flowers o the countryside had arrived. Poppies, Mayweed, varieties of Clover and Buttercup, the enormous Dandelion family, Hemp Agrimony and Rosebay Willowherb, with its glorious pink flowers in striking contrast to the blue water of the lakes. Yarrow, Ragwort and a myriad of grasses hid the pebbles and the effect was that of a great meadow.

Other plants which grew surprisingly well were Teazel, Great Mullein, Fennel and even Dog Rose. Needless to say the Buddleia was not going to be left out and there it was, a scattered bush here and there. Common Toadflax and Purple Toadflax were quite at home as was Lady's Bedstraw, Wall Rocket and the low growing Woody Nightshade.

Every day there was something new to see and often to find that the names of wild flowers belied their appearance. Wild Cabbage sounds mundanely vegetable but it is a lovely plant with clear yellow flowers massed together on tall stems. Hoary Cress likes to grow near the sea. It is an attractive plant with slender green leaves and a cloudy mist of white flower heads.

Behind the coastguard tower on the Point a great mound of dumped material became covered in vegetation. Elder, bramble, grasses, a thriving colony of sea loving Alexanders, Hoary Cress and Teazel rampaged across the once unlovely dumping ground. Plants of the woodland and hedgerow such as violets, Primroses and bluebells, found a place and grew well within a stone's throw of the sea.

The shingle area which remains south of Prince William Parade

Flowers in abundance in a sheltered ridge near the Pevensey border…

retains part of the old ridges and has an interesting variety of maritime flora. Banks on its southern boundary of earth mixed with shingle encourage many wild flowers of the countryside including Migonette, Vetch, and a good range of the Brassicas and Mustards which give a splendid display of yellow in early summer.

English Stonecrop grows here and small heath communities of lichen thrive on the shingle. Yellow Horned Poppy and Bugloss are also abundant as is Sea Kale and Sea Campion, making this open area very attractive in the summer months.

Behind the northern lake on the site of the new Mariners Walk existed another part of the Crumbles which had been used for dumping earth on top of the shingle. Willow, Elder, bramble and wild rose fringed the lake and the path became a countryside walk. Red and White Campion, Comfrey and the brilliant blue flowers of Green Alkanet grew freely and Wood Vetch and Tufted Vetch gave a show of pale mauve, deep mauve or white flowers, thick on each stem.

…Ox eye Daisies in even more abundance.

A shingle garden in high summer. In bloom are Vipers Bugloss, Wild Mignonette, Wild Carrot and the Yellow Horned Poppy.

Colonies of Bee Orchid were established and all along the path Mayweed and Teazel, Musk Thistle and Ragwort grew. Fennel, Great Mullein, White Deadnettle, all had their place, together with some garden escapes, great mauve Opium Poppies and a lone Laburnum tree.

The flowers of the Crumbles were a continuing pageant and in late summer Carline Thistle could be found, its small pale gold flower heads blending so well with the ground they were often glimpsed by chance. This perhaps was the secret of the extraordinary appeal of the Crumbles flora. So much was unexpected but all of it was beautiful.

4. THE FAUNA

Insects inhabit a world in miniature in a tremendous diversity
of form. At least seventy species of spiders lived on the
Crumbles, most of them small and several quite rare. The
splendidly named Myrmarachne formiacera measures only six
millimetres and is a jumping spider with long legs which can
mimic ants and preys on other insects. The males have large
jaws and fight each other for territory, charging like rutting deer.

This aggressive species was abundant on the Crumbles as were
two other jumping spiders, *Sitticus rupicola*, handsomely turned out
with a thick growth of light grey hairs on its sides and a smart
chevron marking on its back, and the extremely rare in Britain
Pellenes tripunctalis, a little black spider with white markings.

Hunting spiders like warm sunny places and are only active in
sunshine. Although many species hibernate in winter they also
make a small webbed cell-like little room to retire to on dull days

Sitticus rupicola, a little jumping spider with chevron markings on his back, was, and maybe still is a Crumbles resident. Photo: E. Jones.

in summer. Also enjoying life on the Crumbles was the aptly named Zebra Spider, *Salticus scenicus*, which had black and white stripes on legs and body. Another resident was the tiny two millimetres long black *Hahnia nava*.

A total of 114 species of beetles have been recorded in the area. They include thirty one species of ground beetles, eight different water beetles, also leaf beetles, small ant-like beetles and three types of ladybird. There were also twenty species of rove beetles and two click beetles. Many of the Crumbles beetle population was common locally but some were rare, including a click beetle *Trixagus obtusus*.

Crickets and grasshoppers are stout insects with large hind legs for jumping and the grasses and warm habitat ensured the Crumbles' share of these busy insects, reported as 'very noisy' near Pevensey. Five species were particularly noted, among them the Grey Bush Cricket which is mainly restricted to the south in England.

Calm warm weather brought the dragonflies out in force. Damsel flies were plentiful in the grasses and near the lakes. Smaller and more delicate than their larger cousins, the slender body of the common kind is a brilliant turquoise blue with black markings.

Although there is no real scientific distinction between them it can be said that generally butterflies are day flying and moths with some exceptions, are nocturnal. Certainly butterflies have the most striking colours and wing patterns provided by minute scales on the membrane but moths have their own charm in many subtle variations.

Well over 200 species of butterflies and moths were recorded on the Crumbles and no doubt many more remained undetected. The Sussex Emerald, a very rare species, was reported in the 1950s and again in the 1970s. Of particular interest was the Toadflax Brocade, established comparatively recently in this country, the larvae feeding on both the Yellow and Purple Toadflax.

Plants of the downland that thrived on the Crumbles attracted the Chalkhill Blue and of the rare and local species one of the most fascinating was the Tawny Shears, *Hadena perplexa*, a small moth with a pretty wing pattern usually of brown and white. It was common on the Crumbles, particularly where there was Sea

Campion, and had developed an almost pure white form.

This was also a locality in which migrant butterflies gained a temporary foothold in this country. They included the Bordered Straw, the Vestal, the Hummingbird Hawk Moth and the Clouded Yellow.

The first days of summer still bring a flock of Large Whites making their landfall after flying across the sea from France. The Red Admiral, Small Tortoiseshell and the Peacock are seen every year and all the butterflies played their part in the colourful scene of sunny days.

BIRDS

The bird population of the Crumbles was at its peak in the early part of the last century. Eastbourne Natural History Society's Notes for 1914 record that their watcher had begun his duties in March and commented on a season that would make the bird watcher of today green with envy.

Snipe, kestrel, kingfisher, peregrine falcon, partridge, redshank, whimbrel, yellow wagtail, nightingale, reed bunting and widgeon were part of the list together with a host of shore waders. However, the watcher also reported: 'Men and boys in search of eggs were met with and the worst ones I wrote warning letters to'. In spite of this the nesting season was a good one.

Human intervention continued to be a threat. A book published in 1930 entitled *A Bird Collectors Medley*, devotes a chapter to the Crumbles and the author, E.C. Arnold, enthused: 'The study of Ornithology may indeed be said to have been brought up to date when you can be transported to the scene of your researches in a motor bus! Yet to this climax of perfection has Eastbourne attained. Its motor bus will land you within five minutes walk from the Crumbles – that is to say within five minutes of one of the best hunting grounds in the whole of the British Isles'.

He goes on to say that 'bushes as might shelter any Warbler under the sun... and there are nests of Plovers, Lapwing and Redshank on the shingle'.

Alas for the sensibilities of today's bird lovers. Mr. Arnold was a collector of both eggs and birds and he shot the birds so they could be set up by the taxidermist and displayed in glass cases. 'It is a case of first come first served,' he writes. 'The first arrival shoots the place out in about an hour' and he gaily goes on, 'it is just the place for the Dusky Redshank and the Wood Sandpiper... I myself once got a Red-necked Phalarope'.

Fortunately it was not always plain sailing for the guns. Mr. Arnold found a disadvantage of the Crumbles was the blackberry gatherers. 'I have found it next to impossible to let off a gun at that season in the bushes' he complains.

By today's environmental considerations this is all very shocking but Mr. Arnold was a man of his time, convinced that collecting specimens was important and there so many birds about it must have seemed to him that a few less would hardly matter.

The birds and their habitat are described with real enthusiasm in his book, and he records a Pratincole, a Grey Phalarope and a Spotted Crake in 1903 and a Glossy Ibis in 1906.

The reed beds were lost when further building took place but the areas east of Langney Point retained a succession of bird life. Cover was sufficient for nesting and also a landfall for tired migrant birds arriving in the spring.

From about 1970 the naturalised lakes attracted a number of water birds. In the 1960s the little tern, black headed gull, common tern and redshank nested there, as did the wheatear, black redstart, linnet and ringed plover in succeeding years.

The Little Ringed Plover

Later records include the short-eared owl, Dartford warbler, snow bunting, tawny pipit, aquatic warbler, great spotted woodpecker, snow robin, bearded tit and Britain's smallest bird, the exquisite goldcrest.

The beautifully marked Little Ringed Plover was well in evidence in the 1980s, its call notes of a regular 'peep peep peep' quite unmistakeable. These small birds are similar in plumage and markings to the larger ringed plover, with light brown plumage above, a white chest and head and well defined black neckband and black band behind the eyes and on the forehead. They only came to live in Britain during the last sixty years and they bred on the shingle and nested on the banks of the lakes.

The lakes had a resident population in the summer months of coot, moorhen, mallard and Great Crested Grebe. These beautiful birds nest exclusively on inland stretches of fresh water and during the 1980's several pairs bred on the northern lake of the Crumbles, the chicks looked after by both parents and often hitching a ride in the plumage on their backs.

Birds that fly south to Britain to escape the Arctic cold were once a feature of the Crumbles lakes. The Scaup was a regular visitor and sometimes the Long Tailed Duck, very smart in appearance with plumage of pale buff and white, a long thin tail and black back. The Smew, once known as the White Nun because of its white plumage with black markings, is the smallest of the saw-billed ducks. The Slavonian Grebe was another winter visitor in its seasonal plumage of black cap and white cheeks, together with the Gadwall – a goose with grey and brown plumage – and the Shoveler, a duck with an enormous bill.

REPTILES AND MAMMALS

Grass snakes were common east of Langney Point and of the amphibians the Smooth Newt bred on the Crumbles, hibernating in winter under a convenient large stone. The lakes provided a home for frogs and toads and the common lizard blended perfectly with the stony ground, a good defence against the predators.

Of the small animals there was a good population of rabbits and also the tiny velvety vole and the field mouse. For some years a large hare was in residence, often seen in the middle area of the Horseshoe Lake.

Foxes found the area an excellent hunting ground. As late as the 1980's they were still breeding there and a small family of cubs which came out to play every evening gave great pleasure to people walking up to the Point. Even now a fox is sometimes seen on his nocturnal prowls there.

Humans used the Crumbles for walks, for fishing, for picking flowers and blackberries and for birdwatching. It was a friendly place with a great deal of space and a wonderful view from the shore to the Downs. For years it was possible to share with the other fauna that lived there the long golden stretches of beachland and grasses, a place where time did not matter, where the senses were sharpened and deeply satisfied by the signs and sounds of a wild and unique area of open land.

5. WHAT OF THE FUTURE?

During the last century the Crumbles has changed beyond recognition as urban development has encroached on the open land. However, human interference has also halted the erosion of the shoreline by erecting sea defences.

The value of the shingle habitat, which is becoming increasingly rare in Britain and Europe, was not recognised until recently, and too late for a survey before development, when it is probable that the Crumbles would have attained the status of an area of special scientific interest. This would have ensured a reasonable degree of conservation.

The loss of the Crumbles habitat may seem insignificant compared to the destruction of the Amazon rain forest but the principle is the same. Where and when should a line be drawn?

The importance of this issue both from an aesthetic point of view and indeed for the survival of the human race is understood in theory but not so easy to put into practice as populations increase and local interests, both economic and social, remain an over-riding factor.

For the future it must be accepted that the Crumbles will be almost completely urbanised . The developers are aware of the special nature of this land and have promised to liaise with the County Ecologist and English Nature who are keen to achieve some small measure of conservation.

A nature reserve is to be kept east of the Sovereign Centre on land owned by the town council. It is an important area of shingle where part of the original ridges, c.1700, will be preserved together with the flora and fauna typical of the old Crumbles land.

It is difficult to imagine the future scene of the Crumbles. Even now on the new housing estates are echoes of the past in the form of such plants as the brilliant Sedum Acre which keeps a hold on pavement edges and gardens and the Red Valerian, pictured below, which appears as if by magic. Swans fly overhead still, cormorants are seen in the marina, migrating birds still use the small spit of land by the outer harbour, and on a still night there is always the muted thunder of the sea on the shingle shore.

All is change and that of course is part of life itself. What will be here at the end of the next thousand years? Anything is possible but one thing is certain. Nature will have the last word.

BIBLIOGRAPHY

Local Martello Towers by H.D. Spears, pamphlet, 1974

Martello Towers by S. Sutcliffe. David and Charles 1972

Norway Notes by V. Miller, pamphlet, 1986.

The Place Names of Sussex by A.Mawyer, F.N. Stenton and J.E.B. Gover

Emglish Place Name Society, Cambridge University Press 1969

The Scarecrow's Legion by G. Hufton and E. Baird, Rochester Press 1983

An Illustrated History of Pevensey by E. Stuart. Pevensey Town Trust

Walls-end- Pevensey Bay by T. McCall, 1983

Lords and Landlords. The Aristocracy and the Towns 1774-1967 by D. Cannadine, Leicester University Press

The Ballast Line. Article by S.C. Nash in The Railway Magazine, 1972

Eastbourne Aviation Company 1911-1924 Pamphlet by H.M. Goodall 1979

The Trial of Field and Gray by W. Duke. William Hodge 1959

Sussex Murders by David Briffet. Countryside Books 1990

Wartime Eastbourne by George Humphrey. Becket Features 1989

NATURAL HISTORY

Coastal Sedimentation in East Sussex during the Holocene. Paper by Dr. Simon Jennings and Christine Smyth 1987

Southeast and Southern England by David Jones. 1981

Environmental Survey on the Crumbles by Hugh Ellacott; Tecnitas U.K. 1988

An Entomological History of the Crumbles by Mark Hadley. Proceedings and Transactions of the British Entomological Natural History Society 1983

ACKNOWLEDGEMENTS

THE author is indebted to the many people who have given help and encouragement in the research undertaken for this book and for the kind permission given for the use of valuable photographs from the Towner Art Gallery, Eastbourne Library, E. Tompsett, Evan Jones and the Eastbourne Gazette.

Special thanks to the staff of the reference section of Eastbourne Central Library, especially Team Librarian Alan Hibbs, without whose generous support this book would never have begun. In the natural history research I was helped greatly to extend my amateur knowledge of the shingle habitat by Evan Jones of Westham who is the true expert on the subject, and also by Hugh Ellacott of Tecnitas UK, Mark Hadley, Chris Durell of English Nature, Susan Wilson of the Sussex Wildlife Trust and Dr. Simon Jennings and Christine Smyth whose paper on coastal sedimentation was an inspiration in itself.

My grateful thanks to you all.